Ṣedeq and Ṣedaqah
in the Hebrew Bible

American University Studies

Series VII
Theology and Religion
Vol. 78

PETER LANG
New York · San Francisco · Bern
Frankfurt am Main · Paris · London

Ahuva Ho

Ṣedeq and Ṣedaqah
in the Hebrew Bible

PETER LANG
New York · San Francisco · Bern
Frankfurt am Main · Paris · London

Library of Congress Cataloging-in-Publication Data

Ho, Ahuva
    Ṣedeq and Ṣedaqah in the Hebrew Bible / Ahuva Ho.
        p. cm. — (American university studies. Series VII,
Theology and religion ; v. 78)
        Includes bibliographical references.
        1. Tsedek (The Hebrew word)   2. Tsedakah
(The Hebrew word)   3. Bible, O.T.—Language, style.
I. Title.   II. Series.
BS1185.H62   1991   221.4'4—dc20   90-19404
ISBN 0-8204-1349-6   CIP
ISSN 0740-0446

CIP-Titelaufnahme der Deutschen Bibliothek

Ho, Ahuva
Ṣedeq and Ṣedaqah in the Hebrew Bible / Ahuva Ho.—
New York; Bern; Frankfurt am Main; Paris: Lang, 1991
    (American university studies : Ser. 7, Theology and
    religion ; Vol. 78)
    ISBN 0-8204-1349-6
NE: American university studies / 07

Printed in the United States of America.

To my father,
Haim Ofri,
the frustrated Bible Scholar,
my model.

מִכָּל מְלַמְּדַי הִשְׂכַּלְתִּי

(תהי קי"ט:צ"ט)

I have learned much from all my teachers.
(Ps. 119:99)

TABLE OF CONTENTS

LIST OF TABLES

ACKNOWLEDGMENTS

This journey through an in-depth philological research into the Hebrew Bible could not have been taken without the encouragement and limitless support of my teacher, Dr. Zioni Zevit, the head of the department of Bible at the Graduate School of the University of Judaism in Los Angeles. His vast erudition in the Bible and Semitic languages, especially Ugaritic, has greatly inspired me to seek for more and more knowledge. It also left me frustrated having realized how little I knew in view of the massive thousands-of-years Jewish creativity.

He taught me to approach a text with an acute observation to detail and with sensitivity to content, as well as to philological, literary, social, historical and comparative awareness. With his methodical and critical research, he taught me to develop my own ideas, even to dismiss and rebut well accepted and revered theories when found wrong.

My ever-lasting, deep love and respect go to my deceased father, Haim Ofri, who since early childhood instilled in me the love and reverence for the Hebrew Scriptures and much pride in my Jewish tradition. His steadfast and unwavering faith in me throughout my life has always sustained me in difficult times. For this and more I am forever grateful.

My thanks go to the rest of my family: To my husband, Dr. Winston G. Ho, whose support, encouragement and love for the last 26 years have helped me to grow. To my children, Harel, Claire and Ofer, whose love and pride have helped me overcome my guilt of failing to be a perfect mother.

INTRODUCTION

In his book *Comparative Philology and the Text of the Old Testament,* James Barr outlines the methods of philological research. He dismisses the overemphasis of scholars on etymology. The meaning of a word has to be sought in its own language. The existence of a similar root in another language does not assure its application to the Hebrew root.[1]

Languages, which evolve from an original source, drift and change.[2] Stephen Ullmann shows the importance of two phenomena on a language: borrowing from another language and the influence of thought upon language.[3] The same word can mean different things in various settings (legal, religious, ethical, etc.) or in different books or genres.[4]

When we encounter a difficult word, analogy may be helpful in determining its meaning. First, the various meanings of a cognate word are compared with the word in question. For example, *bṭḥ* (feel safe) is related to Arabic *baṭaḥa;* *baṭaḥa* also means 'fall down', 'lie down'. Then a search should be made to see if indeed *bṭḥ* in another context has the second meaning, as indeed it does in Jer. 12:5 and in Job 40:25.[5] However, Barr warns against relying too heavily on dictionaries and lexicons. These can be inaccurate and misleading.

John Sawyer also suggests caution when looking for an Arabic support, since this language is "least conservative in its lexicon." Words which can be compared phonologically as cognates with Hebrew have drifted so far from their common meaning, that any support from them is useless. Ugaritic is more stable in its chronological changes[6] and thus more useful for this study, as will be demonstrated below.

However, as Shlomo Morag asserts, Ugaritic texts sometimes distract us from understanding the Biblical Hebrew. Like Barr, he prefers to examine a Hebrew word or locution through similar or parallel cases.[7] Often, when we encounter a unique or controversial word, resorting to cognates is unavoidable, as Yitzhak Avishur shows.[8]

Based on Barr's work, Sawyer suggests three approaches in examining the meaning of a word:[9]

1. CONTEXT: The immediate linguistic environment. For example, *yšb 'l* (sit on) is different from *yšb b-* (dwell); the wider literary context, e.g. genre, book, chapter, unit, style; how thought and history influenced the language; the whole Bible as against post-biblical usage; non-verbal context: how historical events, especially theology, have changed the meaning of the written word.

2. SEMANTIC FIELDS: The associative field of a word is examined, i.e. the terms that accompany the word (verbs, nouns, prepositions: *'śh ṣdq, mšpt ṣdq*);[10] synonyms (צֶדֶק-צְדָקָה), antonyms (צֶדֶק-רֶשַׁע). Are they peculiar to theological, legal, psychological, stylistic or other contexts?

3. ETYMOLOGY: How the semantic content of a word changes through time, usage, etc. to have other meanings in various contexts. We search for the original meaning only in cases of hapax legomena or corrupt texts. Here, phenomena like polysemy, homonymy, extension or restriction of meaning, analogy, metaphorical transferences, loan-words, taboo words, etc. should be considered. Ullmann adds to these 'emotive overtones' which are "words used to express or excite feelings and attitudes."[11]

Leonard Bloomfield, on one hand, declares that "there are no actual synonyms," since forms vary phonemically. Each form serves a specific meaning.[12] Ullmann, on the other hand, finds that synonymy is endemic in legal, technical and scientific spheres. However, he adds that "very few words are completely synonymous in the sense of being interchangeable in any context without the slightest alteration in objective meaning, feeling-tone or evocative value." Sometimes the reason for using a synonym is unknown. This results in misunderstanding and ambiguity.[13]

Unlike Barr, who emphasizes the synchronic approach, Sawyer assigns etymological and historical (diachronic) considerations an important role in semantic research.

This is what all dictionaries and lexicons do. BDB, Koehler-Baumgartner and others classify their work according to roots in an alphabetical order. Etymology comes first. They base their meanings on other dictionaries and lexicons, on parallelism or opposites in other Semitic literatures. Verbs are classified according to stems. Nouns are classified according to meaning and situation-in-life. In the case of homonyms the various "origins" are introduced at the beginning of the entry.[14] Usually, dictionaries and lexicons suggest bibliography at the end of the entry. They also refer to translations such as Targum, Symmachus, LXX and others.

There are many difficulties that stand in the way of the modern historical dictionary writers, because of the lack of semantic guidelines for the delimitation of polysemy and homonymy. Zeev Ben-Haim suggests that only the phonological guideline can be reliably classified. However, in order to do a semantic examination of the Hebrew language, it is preferable to examine the root. This is a difficult task that calls for caution, since we have no criterion to separate polysemy from homonymy.[15]

In almost all investigations of a word in the Theological Dictionary of the Old Testament (TDOT), authors start with an investigation of its original meaning through etymological survey.[16] The examination itself is done mostly by sub-categorizations according to subjects, e.g. various covenants (*b^erith*), various signs ('oth). Popular categorizations are the secular and theological-ritual-religious aspects of the word and the actual and symbolic-metaphoric-figurative usages.

Philological works, in the main, exhibit two principal methods, and both are contextually based. In both methods the word is examined within the context and relationship with its semantic field. Etymology is briefly mentioned.

One method uses pre-conceived categories. Passages are brought as evidence. For example, in a Ph.D. dissertation by Alexander To Ha Luc the word '*hb* is examined. Each sphere of 'love' is a category, e.g.: love between man and woman, between man and God, between parent and child, etc. This approach focuses on a specific category. The choice of category is by content, not genre, author, book or development. The conclusions are stated at the outset of each category, while the text itself is brought for support.

He also quotes other Semitic literature in which the word means the same as in that particular Biblical passage. This method can go beyond the immediate purpose by looking for other synonyms or associative fields, which may not be comparable, because they are indirectly related to the idea of the category. For example, when dealing with love among friends, words like *r'h* (be a friend of) are included.

Also, in his examination of previous studies, Luc brings out the difficulties he finds in them, allowing us to foresee the problems and how he will deal with them. For instance, the division between the secular and theological meaning of love, or the synonyms for '*hb* and their relationship to each other. He refutes the conclusions of past works before stating his own conclusions, which are discussed in more detail later. What we see is the finish of a long research at the opening of each category.

Luc's method is effective and simple. But we are left with no excitement for the end results, since they are already outlined at the start. Also, deep contextual study seems to be secondary.

Maxwell J. Miller is more concise in his approach to the words *ṣelem* and *d˚mut* in Gen. 1:26-27.[18] He investigates the various Biblical passages where these words appear. His method is exclusively contextual. His main concern is to determine the reason behind these usages by P. For this purpose etymological and semantical considerations are unnecessary. In order to answer his question he compares the P creation theology with that of the Mesopotamian tradition of the creation of man. This approach suits the purpose because his research is limited to a specific idea.[19]

The second method is by examination of each occurrence before drawing any conclusions. This work is tedious and difficult and at the same time more textual and exciting because conclusions have not yet been conceived.

Such a method is used by John Olley.[20] He divides his work into two parts: verb forms and noun forms. In each part he first presents the passage and then examines the meaning through discussion of its semantic range of parallels and opposites. The discussion also quotes commentaries of other scholars. He explains the setting and meaning of the whole unit. The reader follows the examination in its slow pace and finds the meaning summarized at the end of each discussion. Etymology is less important.

This is the method I have chosen: a methodical, contextual study with no pre-assumptions. The words צֶדֶק and צְדָקָה will be examined in their context according to genre, units and books, with an effort to find historical development.

My work is divided into three main parts. The first part is devoted to previous research which includes etymology. The second and main part is my research through a thorough contextual examination. The third part sums up the research and draws conclusions.

This work is organized chronologically. The texts are divided according to their genre: narrative, wisdom and prophetic literatures. In each genre צֶדֶק and צְדָקָה are examined. Each chapter will be summarized.

The purpose of this study is to elucidate these two terms from a semantic point of view, to examine their meaning through time, situation-in-life and the methods discussed above. Do they mean the same or do they vary? Did they change? How are they used in different situations? What influenced the choice of one or the other?

Before going into the first part, some thoughts have to be brought up regarding translation.

Biblical Hebrew has changed and evolved during centuries of usage. Dialects developed. Hosea's language is slightly different than Amos' Hebrew. There are words and idioms found only in Hosea, the prophet from the northern kingdom. Although a Hebrew-speaking child of modern Israel can easily read Biblical Hebrew, still there are many words and phrases that lost their original meaning, are unknown today, or acquired a new meaning.

When we try to translate from Biblical Hebrew to another language it becomes a somewhat difficult task. Not only that words and phrases have lost their original meaning, finding an exact equivalent in another language is inadequate. This is more so when the language is not part of the Semitic group but of utterly different thought, logic, and grammar. The multiple translations of the Hebrew Bible into English throughout the centuries is a good testimony.

It is one thing to translate from, say, Hebrew to Aramaic, than from Hebrew to English. This task, in this study, had to be accomplished more through the explanation and elucidation of the text rather than through direct translation of a certain word or phrase. The meaning of the idea, the thought, the philosophy of the language had to have priority in this study.

Parts of a Hebrew sentence are not always synonymous with the same parts in the other language. For example, a verb in Hebrew may be translated as a noun or as an adverb in English; when in English a preposition is used but not in Hebrew, commentators might be inclined to emend the text. This I have seen much too often in Biblical research.

Hebrew has a very different logic and structure than English, French or German, the three languages that are most used in Biblical research. Exegetes must be aware of this reality before trying to find an exact equivalent in their respective language. To emend or dismiss a text based on *their* language does disservice to scholarly studies.

Another problem I have encountered through my research is that in certain cases the set of beliefs of the commentator influences his understanding of the text, and consequently he reaches an inaccurate and erroneous conclusion. This may be either done consciously or subconsciously.

The word "Bible" in this study refers only to the Hebrew Scriptures.

Notes and Abbreviations will appear at the end of this study.

1

ṢDQ/ṢDQH
IN EXTRA-BIBLICAL RESEARCH

The root *ṣdq* can be traced in every west-Semitic language, from South Arabia, through Canaan and Phoenicia to Mesopotamia (the Aramaic influence of Akkadian). It developed various meanings, connotations and technical terms, so that George Cooke could refer to "the wide range of nuances underlying the root."[1]

Norman Snaith sees the basic meaning of *ṣdq* in Arabic *ṣadqun* 'straight,' and opposes it to the basic meaning of *rš'* 'loose,' 'slack.'[2]

In contrast to Snaith, C.F. Whitley, based on Lane's Lexicon, understands the Arabic *ṣadqun* as "true in hardness and strength and goodness" when applied to persons. It also means 'straight' when not relating to persons.[3] Whitley also makes these observations:

1. Abdi-Ḥepa, in his letter to Akhenaten in Amarna,[4] pronounces himself to be right about Milkilu and the sons of Labayu "who have given the land of the king [of Egypt] to the Apiru."[5] He says "ṣa-du-uq ana." Although the letter is written in Akkadian, he uses a west-Semitic word. The root *ṣdq* became a legal, technical word for 'being loyal.'

2. In Ugaritic texts the noun *ṣdq* appears as 'right' or 'uprightness.' The adjective means 'lawful' or 'rightful.'[6]

3. In Phoenician texts *ṣdq* has the meaning of 'legitimacy' as well as 'righteousness.'

4. Aramaic *ṣidqah* means 'righteousness'[7] and the adjective means 'righteous'

or 'just.'[8]

From the above Whitley concludes that *ṣdq* in west-Semitic languages means 'what is right,' 'righteousness,' 'what is true.'[9]

H. Schmid finds that the root *ṣdq* in Hebrew and Canaanite usage was related to kingship ideology, where the king was regarded as the son or representative of the deity.[10]

Similarly, some scholars define *ṣdq* as 'legitimate.' They base their conclusion on Phoenician inscriptions: in a 3rd century BCE inscription from Cyprus, Yathan-ba'al calls Ptolemey II *ṣmh ṣdq*. Since Ptolemey's claim to the throne was disputed, scholars read here a term which validates his kingship. Thus Cooke translates 'legitimate offspring.'[11]

It has the same meaning in Ugaritic in King KRT story of 14th century BCE, where it says:

'aṭt ṣdqh lypq - his legitimate wife did he find

mtrḫt yšrh - even his rightful spouse.[12]

John Gray sees *ṣdq* and *yšr* as technical terms for 'legitimacy.' He bases his translation on the Phoenician inscription of Yeḥimilk of Byblos as translated by M. Dunand,[13] and the inscription of Yeḥawmilk of Byblos according to Cooke.[14] It seems that the House of KRT found it very important to emphasize the legitimacy of the queen, and through her, the legitimacy of her successor.

The Yeḥimilk inscription, dated in the 10th century BCE, lines 3-7, reads:

יארך בעל שמם ובעל <ת>

גבל ומפחרת אל גבל

קדשם ימת יחמלך ושנתו

על גבל כמלך צדק ומלך

ישר לפני אל גבל ק<ד>שם<>.

William F. Albright translates: 'a rightful king and a true king.'[15]

James Swetnam sees *ṣdq* in all these examples as 'legitimate.' He mentions also another Aramaic inscription of Bar-Rekub where the king says (lines 4-7):

בצדק אבי ובצד

כן הושבני מראי רכבאל

ומראי תגלת פלאסר על

כרסא אבי.[16]

Bar-Rekub finds it very important to underline not only his own legitimacy to the throne, but his father's as well. *Ṣdq,* then, is used to designate the legal right to the throne.

The term *bn ṣdq* was found frequently in building inscriptions in Sidon of 300 BCE and Swetnam translates it: 'legitimate heir.'[17]

Julian Oberman understands *ṣdq* as 'loyalty' "corresponding to the usage of *ṣidq* elsewhere in Semitic." He quotes the above inscriptions and translates *'aṭt ṣdqh* as 'his loyal wife.'[18]

Swetnam finds support for *ṣdq* as 'legitimate' in the Bible, in Jeremiah's words צמח צדיק (23:5a and its parallel צמח צדקה in 33:15). It seems that even after Jehoiachin was exiled, he was regarded as the legitimate king. Jeremiah's words come to emphasize this point.[19]

Mitchell Dahood also interprets *ṣdq* as 'legitimate' when he deals with Prov. 8:6 שפטי צדק ('legitimate rulers'). He says that "Northern Semitic usage confirms this exegesis of *ṣedeq*; in Ugaritic and in Phoenician *ṣdq* denoted legitimacy."[21]

Alexander R. Gordon says that צדק or צדקה are connected with Arabic *ṣidq*: 'truth,' 'sincerity,' 'firmness.' צדק/ה means what is trustworthy and what fits its purpose, e.g., the sword that fits its function in battle, or the eye that sees well. It can refer to people, parts of the body, things or actions of man.[21]

Roy Rosenberg explains the Hebrew צדק by exploring other west-Semitic languages. According to him, the root *ṣdq* in South Arabia meant 'that which is proper' or 'that which one deserves.' From this meaning he concludes that *'aṭt ṣdqh* of KRT means 'his rightful wife.' *Ṣmh ṣdq,* then, will be 'rightful offspring.' Yeḥimilk asks for long life because he is 'a righteous king.' Thus Rosenberg sees no difference between 'rightful' and 'righteous.'[22]

BDB gives varied meanings of the Arabic *ṣdq*: 'speak the truth,' 'hard,' 'even,' 'straight' and 'perfect.' In Phoenician the adjective *ṣdq* means 'just,' 'right.' In Old Aramaic the noun *ṣdq* means 'righteousness,' 'loyalty.' *Ṣdq* as a noun can mean 'what is just,' 'normal' and 'right.' On this basis BDB sees Biblical Hebrew צדק as 'righteous' or 'righteousness' in legal matters as well as what is ethically right in general.

Snaith defines צדק as that which God created as a standard norm to be carried out by man. צדק/ה is the nature of God, which encompasses not only justice but other ethical behavior such as charity, mercy, love and pity toward the needy. The established צדק is what is proper, straight, steady and unchangeable. צדק is not an idea but it represents concrete sets of behavior.[23]

Summary: From different west-Semitic literature *ṣdq* seems to have various meanings. When it relates to people it refers to ethical values: what is straight, true, right or lawful. When it refers to royalty or leaders, it means legitimate or loyal.

Almost all scholars point to the Arabic as the language that better preserved the basic meaning of *ṣdq*: what is straight in general took the ethical and legal meaning of what is just and lawful.

An exact parallel for 'legitimate' is found in the Bible, when it relates to royalty.

In all languages 'what is right' in society is maintained. *Ṣdq* does not relate to a deity, but only to the human sphere.

There appears to be no difference in the usage of *ṣdq* or *ṣdqh,* at least in Aramaic בצדקתי קדמה (Nerab) and בצדק (Panamu). The phoenician inscriptions use only the masculine form of *ṣdq*. Only Arabic *ṣdq* does not mean 'legitimate' or 'loyal.'

The following tables illustrate the interpretations to *ṣdq* given by the various scholars.

TABLE 1

A. NOUN

Arabic	Ugaritic	Aramaic	Phoenician
firmness	legitimacy	righteousness	legitimacy
truth	uprightness	loyalty	righteousness
	righteousness		

B. ADJECTIVE

Arabic	Canaanite	Ugaritic	Aramaic	Phoenician
straight	righteous	right	righteous	right
hard		upright	rightful	just
true		rightful		
		loyal		

2

צֶדֶק/צְדָקָה
IN BIBLICAL RESEARCH

Most biblical scholars do not recognize any difference in meaning between צֶדֶק and צְדָקָה. As Snaith says: "It is a matter of style or caprice." צְדָקָה is merely the feminine form of צֶדֶק.[1]

Why does the Hebrew need both masculine and feminine forms? Do they convey the same meaning or they differ? Do they complement each other and create a more complete idea, or is it a matter of style in Hebrew?

The noun צֶדֶק, with its inflections, occurs 119 times in the Bible. צְדָקָה, with its inflections, appears 157 times.

Snaith says that "the original significance of the root ts-d-q...is to be straight. The word thus very easily comes to be used as a figure for that which is, or ought to be, firmly established...In human affairs...It stands for that norm in the affairs of the world to which men and things should conform, and by which they can be measured," e.g., balances and weights.[2]

צֶדֶק has an ethical meaning, the right/wrong conduct, although it is not confined solely to this meaning. Passages like Gen. 38:26, Job 9:15,20 refer to the proper conduct of the times. The same explanation pertains to the only case where the nif'al is used וְנִצְדַּק קֹדֶשׁ (Dan. 8:14): 'the Holy Place shall be put right' after it was desecrated.

Snaith also claims that since צְדָקָה and מִשְׁפָּט appear frequently together, it is most natural to associate the meaning of one to the other. He finds that מִשְׁפָּט is the decision according to an original divine instruction (חוֹרָה), the right as established by custom (e.g. 1 Sam. 2:13, 27:11). The 'secular' מִשְׁפָּט reached a higher level. When one does מִשְׁפָּט he performs God's will "as it has been made clear in past experience." And so also צֶדֶק. It is what God established in His world to be the proper manner. It is the tool with which, or the standard by which, He judges the world (Ps. 98:9).

Both מִשְׁפָּט and צֶדֶק are divine ideas to be activated on earth. They are actual deeds. The only difference between מִשְׁפָּט and צֶדֶק is that מִשְׁפָּט remained connected to court and law, while צֶדֶק developed a broader meaning.[3]

Law and ethics are one in the Bible, since both emanate from God. They came to promote justice. Justice, then, is the result of maintaining law and ethics. That is how James Priest describes צֶדֶק.[4]

Herbert Huffmon states that צֶדֶק is "common Semitic, except Akkadian."[5]

צְדָקָה, according to Eliezer Berkovits, is a value in the content of מִשְׁפָּט (Jer. 9:23). This is the proper behavior and action coming from God to be carried out by men. When man is in charge of צְדָקָה then it is any good deed, with no obligation set upon the doer or, simply, 'charity.'[6]

צֶדֶק in Israel, says Gordon, applies mostly to the social sphere. It is the customs and laws of that society. When one adheres to this צֶדֶק, he is צַדִּיק. Later he says that צֶדֶק is the righteousness of God. It is the divine character and will.[7]

Sawyer sees a distinction between צֶדֶק and צְדָקָה. He brings צְדָקָה as an example for words which, in later times, lost their connection to their roots. First צְדָקָה denoted 'righteousness' and later 'almsgiving.' צֶדֶק, as other forensic terms changed in time into the metaphoric sphere of feelings. צֶדֶק, justice, has been extended and applied to non-legal contexts.[8]

According to John Bollier, צֶדֶק is no different from צְדָקָה, its feminine form. It is the common word for 'righteousness.' Meter or sheer caprice seem to be the only reasons for using this word or the other. It can mean legal justice or conforming to certain rules laid down by God. He feels that looking for etymological help from Arabic does not help to shed light on the whole scope of Hebrew צדק.[9]

Elizabeth R. Achtemeier also sees no significant difference between צדק and צדקה. He defines צדק as "a concept of relationship...whether that relationship be with men or with God." In every society there are set demands. Their fulfillment constitutes righteousness. Because of this interpretation, Achtemeier concludes that צדק/ה cannot be translated specifically but can vary in meaning. It all depends on the context. It can mean 'vindication' (Ps. 103:6), 'deliverance' (Isa. 46:12), 'saving deeds' (1 Sam. 12:7) and more.

צדק has a forensic meaning too. It appears with either the verb שפט or the noun משפט (Deut. 25:1, 1 Kgs. 8:32). As Bollier, Achtemeier does not find Arabic ṣdq helpful in shedding light on the understanding of Hebrew צדק.[10]

Through the divine צדק Israel received the law. This was done in order to maintain a balance of rights in society. This connection between צדק, God, the law and Israel, was emphasized by Heinz Schrey.[11]

Edmond Jacob summarizes צדק as "what is normal and customary."[12]

Johannes Pedersen defines צדק with a more philosophical nuance saying that it is "that which is in accord with its being."[13]

Whitley says that צדק/ה is "the many aspects of Yahweh's power and influence."[14]

BDB finds that the basic meaning of צדק/ה is 'rightness' and 'righteousness.'[15]

Yaacov Licht says that there is no use in trying to find a comprehensive definition for צדק, because of the many nuances of its root. Although in many cases צדק and צדקה are synonymous, there is a slight difference between these two words: while צדק can be the ideal to come in the future, divine benevolence (Isa. 45:8, Ps. 85:12), or the abstract idea of justice in court (Deut. 1:16, 16:20), צדקה is appropriate conduct in the present, various proper acts or rights.

צדק is an inclusive concept that has no plural form and thus cannot be detailed. צדקה is an actual, specific act (Deut. 24:13), as well as the overall acts (Ez. 18:24). Both צדק and צדקה refer to righteous, proper conduct as well as to legal matters. Both relate to time and to divine and human spheres.[16]

Although Snaith sees the use of צדק and צדקה as a literary caprice, he says that while צדק encompasses initially the different nuances of justice in legal matters, צדקה gives צדק the ethical side of the idea of justice. This he learns from Ps. 112:9 and Dan. 4:24. In both passages צדקה is connected with giving to the poor. This meaning of צדקה developed in post-biblical Hebrew to mean 'almsgiving,' 'charity.' Thus צדקה went beyond strict justice to show mercy to the poor by giving them concrete help.[17]

This interpretation is discussed by several scholars:

Albert L. Vincent sees a development in Arabic that led צדק into the meaning of 'alms.' This meaning was taken over by Hebrew.[18]

Franz Rosenthal disagrees. In Arabic the root ṣdq means, among other things, some kind of dowry. Ṣadaqah as 'charity' is a loan word from the Hebrew-Aramaic as a result of a historical, and not semantic, development. This borrowing took place only at the beginning of the Islamic era. On the basis of one Aramaic inscription from the 5th century BCE (Tema) he finds that the root ṣdq has the meaning of 'grant' or 'gift.' Hebrew assumed the meaning 'charity' from Aramaic and not from Arabic. Deutero-Isaiah uses צדקה as 'charity' as well as an abstract term.

Dan. 4:24 is another piece of evidence for this influence. Now, in the post-exilic era, all donations sent to Israel for the rebuilding of the Temple and the support of the population, were considered as צדקה. So what was first a term for moral behavior reached its latest development in the meaning of charitable giving.[19]

However, at the outset of his article, Rosenthal says that צדקת ה' may have implied, or been understood, among other things, as an act of charity to the poor.

This meaning, he says, may have influenced Daniel when he used צְדָקָה. This assumption is questionable for two reasons:

1. 'צִדְקֹת ה appears in a very ancient text (Judg. 5:11), and throughout the centuries this phrase is strongly connected with the divine, military saving acts.[20]

2. Daniel's צִדְקָה is Aramaic, and as Rosenthal says later, influenced the Hebrew צְדָקָה much later, to adopt the meaning of 'charity.'

Snaith does not see post-exilic צְדָקָה as the result of the influence of Aramaic צְדָקָה but as an influence of the prophets' ideology. According to the prophets צְדָקָה was more than mere justice. It included the whole aspect of ethics. It meant charity, pity and mercy.[21] However, Snaith does not distinguish between early and late prophets.

So, all in all, Snaith sees צדק/ה as overall ethical behavior, which occurs in all west-Semitic languages. This right conduct also includes justice. צְדָקָה is the extension of צדק—justice—with all its ethical implications.

According to Shalom Spiegel, צדק is "strength by which a social structure is able to maintain itself." צדק is justice, righteousness, which is what is good and healthy to society. צדקה can mean "infinite strength" as in Isa. 45:24, Ps. 71:16-19.[22]

Some scholars find in the Bible traces of צדק having reference to the god *Ṣedeq,* the local god of pre-Davidic Jerusalem. This will be discussed in detail in chapter 5.

Summary: Scholars consider צדק and צדקה either as complete synonyms or as concepts with a slight difference in meaning. All scholars see צדק/ה as ethical concepts. Some would emphasize the legal implication of the word and others—that of proper conduct. All agree that צדק/ה are divine characteristics, or gifts given by the deity to mankind/Israel to be carried out. We thus have a connection between God-ethics-law-society in the concepts of צדק/ה.

Some scholars find a development in meaning. Most of them see the development starting with the 8th century prophets. They all try to understand the meaning of צדק/ה by comparing the Hebrew root with its employment in other west-Semitic languages. Thus the scope of meaning widens from what is straight to what is true, right, proper, the legitimacy of kings, strength, salvation, behavior and justice.

'Righteousness,' one of the translations for צדק or צדקה, belongs initially to the divine sphere. It is a theological concept. When 'righteousness' refers to people, the theological concept is transferred into the human sphere. However, the divine and secular spheres intertwine. That is why scholars, especially the Christian, move from 'righteousness' to 'salvation,' 'victory' and 'justice' with ease.

3
צֶדֶק
IN THE NARRATIVE LITERATURE

צדק in the narrative literature appears five times in the Holiness Code of Leviticus and five times in the Deuteronomic Code of Deuteronomy, and once outside of this code.

Gordon says that Deuteronomy turned the willing pursuit of moral behavior into divine laws: following God's laws of righteousness meant doing His will. Proper behavior was turned into commandments and judgments. The legal form of ethical behavior in society was more crystallized in the Holiness Code and in Ezekiel.[1]

The opening statement of the third group of laws in the Holiness Code (Lev. 19:2b: קדשים תהיו כי קדוש אני ה' אלהיכם) provides the setting for the following laws.[2]

1. LEVITICUS

19:15 - A - לא-תעשו עול במשפט: You shall not do wrong in judgment:

B - לא-תשא פני דל   do not favor the poor

C - ולא תהדר פני גדול;   or show deference to the rich;

D - בצדק תשפט עמיתך.   Judge your neighbor rightly.

Line A opens the clause which is spelled out in the couplet of lines B and C. Line D closes the clause in another general statement, that parallels line A. דל and גדול, עָוֶל and צדק are opposites. Line A refers to the judges and probably the witnesses,[3] while line D refers to each and every judge. While lines A, B and C are negatively declared, line D, the concluding idea, appears in the positive. It is the only criterion for right judging.

Here צדק relates to two specific cases: the prohibition to declare a poor man innocent, because of the pre-conception that being poor means being oppressed and hence a victim; and the prohibition to declare a rich man innocent, because of his status in society. Doing so is עול—wrong. Judging objectively is צדק—right. צדק, then, is what a judge in court should do, the proper behavior of a judge in legal matters.

צדק here is in a social sphere, in a court setting. Judging with צדק keeps the balance in society. Onkelos reads בקשׁטא (in truth). צדק is the means by which the holiness of Israel is maintained. Breaking this holiness defiles the people. This calls for severe punishment (19:, 20:2-3,5-6 and more). This is the first time that צדק is connected with the divine holiness.[4] בצדק is an adverb.

19:35-36 - A - לא-תעשׁו עול במשׁפט: You shall not do wrong in judgment:

   B - במדה במשׁקל ובמשׂורה   in measure of weight and of capacity;

   C - מאזני צדק, אבני-צדק   you shall have a right balance, right weights,

   D - איפת צדק והין צדק יהיה לכם.   a right ephah and a right hin.

The structure of the law proceeds from a general statement to a detailed one without a concluding statement. Line A is the same opening statement as in v. 15. While there it had a clear court setting, here the law refers to weights and measures in a market setting. במשׁפט is an accidental copy from v. 15 and should be deleted.[5] The precept should read לא-תעשׂו עול בַּמִּדָּה, where מדה stands as a general term for what is measured. Then מאזני צדק and הין צדק are the detail of משׁקל. איפת צדק and הין צדק are the detail of משׂורה (a measuring vessel). Again, עָוֶל stands in opposition to צדק, in the meaning of 'honest,' which stands for what is standard. צדק is an adjective.

2. DEUTERONOMY

1:16 - A - ואצוה את שפטיכם   And I charged your judges

     בעת ההיא לאמר: at that time as follows:

B - שְׁמֹעַ בֵּין-אֲחֵיכֶם   Hear out your fellow men,

C - וּשְׁפַטְתֶּם צֶדֶק בֵּין-אִישׁ   and judge rightly between any man

וּבֵין אָחִיו וּבֵין גֵּרוֹ...   and a fellow Israelite or a stranger...

Here too the structure of the verse proceeds from a general statement to a somewhat detailed one. Moses recalls the time when, after appointing judges, he instructed them in their duties (line A is a summation of Exod. 18:13-26) to hear disputes between people in general (line B) and between individuals, including non-Israelites (line C).

Verse 17 goes into further detail. וּשְׁפַטְתֶּם צֶדֶק is similar to תִּשְׁפֹּט בְּצֶדֶק (19:15), but the proposition 'ב' is missing. Similar constructions are found in Ps. 58:2, 67:5, 75:3, and 82:2. וּשְׁפַטְתֶּם צֶדֶק is a stylistic variant for וּשְׁפַטְתֶּם בְּצֶדֶק or צֶדֶק וּשְׁפַטְתֶּם מִשְׁפָּט. צֶדֶק is the means by which the judge maintains order in society. The distributive expression בֵּין...וּבֵין adds to the idea of balance.[6] צֶדֶק functions as an adverb.

16:18 - A - שֹׁפְטִים וְשֹׁטְרִים תִּתֶּן-לְךָ בְּכָל שְׁעָרֶיךָ...   You shall appoint judges and clerks in all your towns...

B - וְשָׁפְטוּ אֶת הָעָם מִשְׁפָּט-צֶדֶק.   and they shall judge the people with a right judgment.

Line A reflects the court setting at the gate. Line B describes the duty of the court personnel: to judge correctly. It again functions as an adjective, just as מֹאזְנֵי צֶדֶק does. It seems that מִשְׁפַּט צֶדֶק is a legal term, like עֵד שֶׁקֶר, עֵד חָמָס or נְשֹׂא פָנִים. It is an expression equivalent to בְּצֶדֶק. Ezekiel and Zechariah use the term מִשְׁפַּט אֱמֶת.[7]

25:15 - אֶבֶן שְׁלֵמָה וָצֶדֶק יִהְיֶה-לָּךְ   You shall have a perfect and right weight

אֵיפָה שְׁלֵמָה וָצֶדֶק יִהְיֶה לָּךְ.   You shall have a perfect and right ephah.

In contrast to the two different sizes of weights and measures (big and small), the law demands only one weight and one measure. 'ו' conjunctive combines two terms: אֶבֶן/אֵיפָה שְׁלֵמָה and אֶבֶן/אֵיפַת צֶדֶק (Lev. 19:36). It may be a Deuteronomic style. צדק is an adjective: the correct standard stone and ephah.[8]

צדק is what is perfect and thus honest. The term שלמה may have been D's own coinage,[9] or the term of his time. Or, it may have come from another source. Another possibility is that D preferred the noun צדק in order to avoid a phrase where masculine and feminine terms clash: צדק (masculine) combined with אבן/איפה (feminine). אבן צדקה is not a legal term.

16:20 - צדק צדק תרדף. Justice (and only) justice you shall pursue.

The repetitive style has a number of functions. Here it serves to emphasize that only צדק, as a general term for what was said before, will be pursued. It appears here as a noun.[10] The repetitive style is a rhetorical means to attract the audience's attention[11] and to emphasize the importance, validity and gravity of the words and ideas. This emphasis helps the audience to remember the key words.

צדק is the right criterion by which a judge conducts a trial. It contrasts with the description in v. 19. צדק prevails when the judge does not distort justice, when he is impartial and when he rejects bribes. צדק prolongs life.

Summary: צדק relates only to legal matters. It is the only criterion by which to conduct a trial. It is a tool with which one knows how to maintain justice and order in society. It is secular, although in the background this behavior and tool are divine in origin. In most cases, it is addressed to the judge.

צדק is the opposite of עול—wrong. It is associated with המשפט (court) and with שפט (to judge), with either its noun or its verb. When it is associated with the market-place, it appears as an adjective where it means 'perfect' (שלם) or 'correct,' 'standard.' In both Leviticus and Deuteronomy this criterion is spelled out. It means being impartial, being above pre-conceptions, pressures and bribes. Leviticus associates צדק with its theological concept of the holiness of Israel and God.

The Leviticus laws, whether secular or religious, were put into the frame-work of Levitical theology: holiness and defilement. Judging according to a set of standard, divine laws became part of the idea of the essence of Adonai, who brought Israel out of Egypt.[12]

Deuteronomy associates צדק with the theological concept of prolonged life and the right to the land (4:1,26, 5:30). The covenant is the framework of D's theology, not holiness (4:31, 5:2-3). It is obvious that D made use of the legal texts of Leviticus (and others), and paraphrased them in his style. Since Deut. 1:16 is in a narrative style, the legal terminology is dropped. It simply says ושפטתם צדק. The genre of exhortation takes the place of the legal genre.

TABLE 2

Right criterion of judge	Adjective: right, just, correct	Adverb: rightly justly	Noun: justice
11	7	2	2

4

צְדָקָה
IN THE NARRATIVE LITERATURE

צדקה appears 20 times in the narrative literature. However, the time span is great: from the 10th century BCE (Sam., Gen.) to the 5th or 4th century BCE (Neh., Chron.). This word will be examined chronologically, starting with Samuel. When parallels occur they will be discussed alongside the original.

1. SAMUEL (Kgs., Chron.)

26:23 - וה' ישב לאיש   Adonai will repay the man his rightness

את צדקתו ואת אמונתו.   his rightness and truthfulness.

David expresses the same idea in poetry in 2 Sam.:[1]

22:21 - יגמלני ה' כצדקתי,   Adonai will reward me according to my rightness,

כבר ידי ישב לי.   He will requite me according to the cleanliness of my

hands.

v. 25 - וישב ה' לי כצדקתי,   And Adonai has requited me according to my

rightness,

כברי לנגד עיניו.   according to my purity in His sight.

צדקה is synonymous with אמונה (truth) and with בּר ידים (cleanliness of hands). They appear in parallel in Ps. 40:11, 143:1.[2] This cleanliness of hands is alluded to, again, in 1 Sam. 26:23 where twice David claims that he did not stretch out his hand to touch Saul.

According to both narrative and poetry accounts David's צדקה means adherence to God's laws. This makes him תמים (perfect) and חסיד (righteous). The reward basically is prolonged life under God's protection (1 Sam. 26:24, 2 Sam. 22:17-20,29-30,33-46,48-49,51). אמונה is one's faithfulness to the law. In poetry צדקה is symbolized by clean hands to indicate purity of actions. In both accounts צדקה is associated with reward by the verbs שוב/שׁב and גמל in hif'il.[3]

Although צדקה is not in a legal context, it is strongly connected with behavior as demanded by law.

2 Sam. 19:29 - ומה-יש-לי עוד צדקה   What right have I

ולזעק עוד אל המלך?   to appeal further to Your Majesty?

Upon returning to his house, David meets Mephibosheth, son of Saul, who admits that even though hostility existed between his father's house and David, David set him among those who ate at his table. As such, Mephibosheth feels no right to call for mercy. זעק אל is to call for help and justice, whether to God or to a king/leader.[4]

Because of the word עוד, David Kimhi,[5] Moshe Segal[6] and Yehuda Keele[7] read: 'how can I ask you for more good deeds?' H.P. Smith translates 'claim.'[8] This 'right' relates to local customs.

2 Sam. 8:18 - ויהי דוד עשה משפט וצדקה   And David executed judgment and

rightness

לכל-עמו.   among all his people.

(1. Chron. 18:14 - ... לכל-עמו. (ויהי עשה משפט וצדקה לכל-עמו.

1 Kgs. 10:9 - וישימך למלך   And he made you king

לעשות משפט וצדקה.   to execute judgment and rightness.

2 Chron. 9:8 - ויתנך עליהם למלך   And He put you over them

לעשות משפט וצדקה.   to execute judgment and rightness.

All passages come right after the statement that David and Solomon ruled over all Israel. The author immediately informs us that David carried out the law. משפט וצדקה (as against צדקה ומשפט) have a definite legal meaning. But why does he add וצדקה? Does it not suffice to say המשפט?

משפט is the case in court, the procedure, the punishment, the execution and, most of all, it is a comprehensive word for the laws themselves. When one does משפט, he carries out the laws as a judge, a defender of the downtrodden, and as a prosecutor.[10]

Because משפט is a general term for justice and its procedure, צדקה is the actualization of the law. While משפט denotes the legal aspects of the law,[11] צדקה is its implementation. That is why it is inadequate to say that one does justice in court. Its implementation closes the circle of justice. The idiom משפט וצדקה underlines the king's adherence to law and order and, thus, to the protection of each citizen. It is consistently associated with עשה (to do), which enhances the idea of performance. 'Judgment and rightness' stand for 'righteous justice.'

2. GENESIS

15:6 - וְהֶאֱמִ֖ן בַּֽה׳   And he believed in Adonai

וַיַּחְשְׁבֶ֥הָ לּ֖וֹ צְדָקָֽה.   and considered it to be His truthfulness.

God promises Avram protection, an heir and numerous progeny. Avram does not doubt Him. He believes in Him and considers it צדקה. What is the object of ויחשבה? The truth or belief (אמונה)?[12] I offer here a new reading without disturbing the characters. I reckon that the 7th-9th century C.E. naqdanim (grammarians) may have vocalized this word erroneously. My reading is וַיַּחְשְׁבֶהָ—'and he thought Him,' or 'considered Him'? From the syntax of this difficult phrase צדק has to be connected with the essence of God: the truthfulness of God, as presented by His promises, was the צדקה for Avram. אמונה (through the verb אמן) is equated with צדקה. There is no legal connotation here.

Rashi sees the subject of ויחשב to be God, who considered Avram's belief to be a merit for Avram. Ramban disagrees and says that it was Avram who believed in God's promises; that through Him the promises will be fulfilled. This צדקה is the truthfulness of God's words.[13]

Abraham Speiser follows Rashi and Onkelos, translating: "He put his trust in

Yahweh, who accounted it to his merit."[14]

Samuel R. Driver sees צדקה as the devotion and trust in God.[15] John Skinner explains it as the "right relation to God conferred by a divine sentence of approval." It is not based on divine law but on inner trust in God.[16]

Let me offer here a more conceivable, likely reading than the one offered above. When we compare our text to Psalms 106:31 a new reading comes forth, which supports Onkelos', Rashi's and Speiser's reading.

In both texts two men are depicted as true believers: Avram "believed" and Phenehas "prayed" to God. In both cases צדקה was granted to them as a reward for their faith. And in both texts it comes with the verb לְ+חשב. The verb appears here in nif'al, making it clear that God is the source of the reward. This is a strong support for emending the reading in Genesis from וַיַּחְשְׁבֶהָ to וַתֵּחָשְׁבָהּ. Avram proved himself to be devout and faithful, to which God responded with a reward of a series of blessings. Consequently, the translation should be: "And he believed in Adonai, so He considered this to be his reward."

It appears that the psalmist knew the Genesis text and incorporated the idiom into his poetry. Based upon this I suggest that the narrative story in Genesis was originally composed in poetry.

18:19 - ושמרו דרך ה' And they shall keep the way of Adonai

לעשות צדקה ומשפט. to do what is right and just.

The one who does צדקה maintains the path of God. צדקה also is associated with משפט. Doing צדקה assures reward, which is the fulfillment of God's promises.

Usually, this verse is regarded as a Deuteronomistic insertion. It reflects the Wisdom philosophy of divine reward for right acts. צדקה is emphasized, the moral behavior, not משפט. דרך ה', משפט and reward are Deuteronomistic in concept and belong to the Wisdom teaching. The use of צדקה ומשפט and not משפט וצדקה points to these sources.

Driver reads 'justice'[17] and Speiser holds to the notion of proper behavior, translating 'what is just.'[18]

30:33 - ועהה בי צדקתי ביום מחר   Let my honesty testify for me in the future,

כי תבא על-שכרי לפניך.   when you go over my wages.

צדקתי is the subject of תבא. Jacob tries to prove to Laban his good, clean character based on his right actions. צדקה is Jacob's evidence and testimony in case Laban, some time in the future, should accuse him of improper actions. So again צדקה refers to proper behavior with no connection to divine laws. It refers to human behavior and to local laws. בא לפני gives צדקה a legal nuance.

Skinner translates 'righteousness,'[19] Driver—'fair dealing,' 'honesty'[20] and Speiser—'honesty.'[21]

3. DEUTERONOMY

6:25 - וצדקה תהיה-לנו   It will be our reward

כי נשמר לעשות את כל המצוה הזאת...   if we observe this whole instruction...

24:13 - ...השב תשיב לו את העבט   You must return the pledge to him...

ולך תהיה צדקה לפני ה' אלהיך.   and you shall have a reward before Adonai.

9:4 - ...אל תאמר בלבבך   Say not to yourselves...

בצדקתי הביאני ה' לרשת את הארץ הזאת.   "because of my rightness Adonai has brought me to inherit this land."

9:5 - לא בצדקתך ובישר לבבך   Not because of your rightness and rectitude

אתה בא לרשת את ארצם...   you will inherit their land...

9:6 - וידעת כי לא בצדקתך   Know, then, that not because of your rightness

ה' אלהיך נתן לך את-הארץ...   Adonai your God is giving you the land...

33:21 - צדקת ה' עשה   He performed the saving acts of Adonai

ומשפטיו עם ישראל.   and (executed) His laws within Israel.

In 6:25 and 24:13 צדקה is the reward Israel will get from God for keeping His commandments. This reward is to inherit Canaan, to overcome all enemies, to have a good life and to survive as a nation (vv. 18-19,24). צדקה is equated with the concept of reward. It will materialize on the basis of a correct relationship between

Israel and God (although this condition is one way).

צדקה will not happen if this relationship is broken. The way for it to be broken is by not observing God's instructions. Again צדקה is conditioned by the word לעשות (to do). It is different here from all that we have seen until now, because here it is what God will do for Israel and not what Israel does. It is the object or the outcome for being obedient to the divine will.[22] The expression in both passages is the same: 'to have צדקה before God,' as a result of observing God's law. This צדקה is connected to Gen. 15:6 only in the idea that it is associated with God's essence.

Gerhard Von Rad translates 'righteousness' which is "a man's correct attitude towards claims which others or another—in this case God—have upon him." צדקה is based on the belief in God.[23]

In Deut. 9:4-6 צדקה stands for the good deeds of Israel (and their 'straightness of heart'), in contrast to the evil deeds of the nations.[24]

33:21 is poetry, the blessing of Gad by Moses. Since צִדְקַת parallels מִשְׁפָּטִיו, and since it always comes in plural with 'ה, it is better to read צִדְקוֹת. צדקת ה' will be discussed in chapter 9.

4. KINGS (Chron.)

The next passages are Deuteronomistic in style and ideas.

1 Kgs. 3:6 - כַּאֲשֶׁר הָלַךְ לְפָנֶיךָ   As he walked before You

באמת ובצדקה...   in truth and in rightness...

There is no משפט here since the author does not touch on David's function as judge, but as a person of moral conduct. One does not 'walk' with the law. Here we have three traits: אמת ('truth'), צדקה ('rightness,' 'right conduct') and ישרת לבב ('straightness of heart,' 'rectitude').[25] צדקה represents the actions while ישרת לבב represents the thoughts. The reward of good actions is the security of a Davidic dynasty (cf. 2 Sam. 22:51).

1 Kgs. 8:32 - להרשיע רשע לתת דרכו בראשו,   To condemn the wicked by bringing

down the punishment of his conduct on his head

ולהצדיק צדיק לתת לו כצדקתו.   and to vindicate the righteous by

rewarding him according to his right conduct.

(2 Chron. 6:23 - להשב לרשע לתת דרכ בראשו,

ולהצדיק צדיק לתת לו כצדקתו.)

דרך is the path of behavior by which God will judge a person, either to pronounce him guilty or innocent. צדקה is the opposite of the 'path of the wicked.' One example is given in which a man takes an oath in court to incriminate an innocent man (v. 31). צדקה of a man is his right actions in accordance with the law. צדיק is the opposite of אשר ירשיע (the sinner who deviates from the law).

The combination of צדקה+ב+נתן is a later, less poetic style than גמל/שוב+ב+ צדקה we have seen in the book of Samuel (J?). The meaning is the same.

God's way is imitated by man. As in other passages, the idea of direct correlation between doing good and reward is present here as well.[26]

5. NEHEMIAH

צדקה appears only once in Nehemiah, in the prophet's reply to his enemies, who were trying to halt the rebuilding of the walls of Jerusalem.

2:20 - ואנחנו עבדיו נקום ובנינו   And we, His servants, will start building,

ולכם אין-חלק וצדקה וזכרון בירושלם.   but you have no share, no right, nor memorial in Jerusalem.

צדקה has the same meaning as in 2 Sam. 19:29—'right.' Nehemiah excludes his opponents from any right to Jerusalem, to Adonai, to His divine plan, to Israel or to the renewal of the religious and political life of Israel. They do not belong to the people of God nor to its destiny.

Ibn Ezra explains that they are not worthy to do good, righteous deeds in building the Temple, so that they will be remembered favorably before God.[27]

Lorin Batten limits this right to political authority over the people of Jerusalem, that may have come from a Persian decree.[28] But this is not so. The Samaritans, represented now by Sanballat, claimed to belong to the religious community of Jerusalem. They wanted to participate in the rebuilding of the Temple in the time of Ezra (4:2). However, this was probably an excuse on the Samaritans' part to have a political hold on Jerusalem.

Summary: צדקה in the narrative literature can be divided into two main spheres: the secular and the religious.

1. Secular: Belonging to an early period, source J uses צדקה to mean the proper behavior and actions of a person according to the local laws and customs (Gen. 30:33). To this we can add Gen. 38:26, when Judah admits that Tamar acted in conformity with custom. צדקה also means 'right' or 'claim.' This meaning continued in use to the time of Nehemiah.

2. Religious: This sphere relates either to man or to God. When צדקה relates to man it is his adherence to God's laws. Source J associates צדקה with אמונה and with בֹּר (cleanliness, mostly of hands), and with שׁב and גמל (both in hif'il). The one who does צדקה is rewarded by God. The reward is divine protection from enemies and misfortunes in life, and consequently prolongs life. צדקה, on the other hand, is God's truthfulness to His promises.

The Deuteronomist equates צדקה with the reward itself, which is connected with obeying the law. The reward is goodness from God and longevity. It also means the good behavior and actions of man. Then it is connected with any proper behavior.

In the Deuteronomistic literature right actions of David result in securing his dynasty. צדקה means the deeds one does in accordance with the law. Source D prefers the style of נתן+צדקה to that of J's (?) שׁב/גמל+צדקה.

Source D also uses two idioms: משׁפט וצדקה, an idiom that relates to kings with the emphasis on the implementation of the law; and צדקה ומשׁפט, an idiom with the emphasis on proper behavior and actions and on morality rather than on the law. The difference at the time, though, was slim as moral behavior was in fact conceived as learnt through God's laws.

Also, both idioms are strongly associated with the verb עָשָׂה, which underlines the importance of doing, rather than the mere knowing or thinking.

Time has given צְדָקָה a stronger emphasis on two factors: its religious association to deeds and its connection to divine reward of security and long, happy life. At the same time its secular meaning of 'right' was retained in use, although quite rarely.

TABLE 3

Right actions and behavior of man	Reward by God	Right, merit	The good essence of God
14	2	2	1

5

צֶדֶק
IN THE WISDOM LITERATURE

In this chapter the word צדק in the books of Psalms, Proverbs, Qoheleth (Ecclesiastes) and Job will be examined.

1. PSALMS

The psalms vary widely in date of composition, in style, in function and in content. It is difficult to look for philological developments, unless there is no doubt about the date of the psalm. In some cases this is impossible to determine.

צדק appears 50 times in Psalms[1] where thirty of them relate to God's activities. The most common phrase is that God judges the world בצדק, באמונה, במישרים and במשפט. The basic idea behind this relation is that God is שפט צדק—'a just judge' (9:5). This expression has become an epithet of God, like הרכב בערבת—'who rides the clouds' (68:5).

17:1 - ;צדק, ה', שמעה   Hear, Adonai, (my) case (plea);

v. 15 - .אני בצדק אחזה פניך   I shall see Your face (as a result of my) right verdict

(vindication). Or,

I shall see Your face rightfully.

These passages are difficult and a satisfactory reading may not be found.

Charles A. Briggs sees צדק as the object of hearing in שמעה צדק ('hear what is right' or 'hear my plea'). He prefers to read צַדִּיק ('hear a righteous man') as in the Latin version of Jerome. He does the same thing in 4:2 where he reads צדיק instead of צִדְקָ.[2]

צדק has to be something audible, since it comes with the verb 'hear.' Ibn Ezra explains this shortened style as if it was written: שמעה ,ה', כי צדק אדבר ('listen, Adonai, for I am speaking the truth' (or, 'rightly,' 'rightfully'). For him, too, צדק is audible. Targum adds an object to שמעה: פגיעתי (my plea), and instead of צדק he reads בצדקה.[3]

The psalmist calls God to judge him. In his opening, he asks God to listen to his case. Then, through רנה ('words of poetry,' 'cry') and תפילה ('prayer') he presents the case in detail. He is certain that after God hears his plea, his משפט ('judgment') and מישרים ('the truth of the case') will clearly be understood and uncovered. צדק, then, may be the case in general or the plea in particular. At the end of the trial, when he is vindicated, he will see God's face בצדק, rightfully.

Or, בצדק is the right verdict, the outcome of the plea—צדק—that opened the psalm (first inclusio).[4] In this way the psalmist uses צדק as two legal terms that open and close a trial, and places them in the psalm in the same order. As a vindicated man he can approach God and envision or experience His essence.

At the basis of צדק in 17:1 and 17:15 lies the belief that the plea and its outcome are righteous. Also, that these are the terms used by the strong believer in God, who is usually the defendant.

Another inclusio in this psalm is found in the word חזה (to see in a. spiritual way). In v. 2 God can see the truth of the case and in v. 15 it is the psalmist who will "see" God as a result of the right verdict. The word בהקיץ ('awake') is not synonymous to בצדק, but adds another idea.[5] Only פניך ('Your face') and תמונתך ('Your vision') are synonymous.

צדק as 'just verdict,' 'vindication,' is found in the following six passages:
40:10 - בשרתי צדק בקהל רב.   I proclaimed just verdicts in great congregations.

This psalm was probably written by an ex-judge, who followed God's laws with utmost conviction. His faithful dedication may have caused his downfall. He proclaimed just verdicts in court, despite pressures from the people in power (הנה

שפטי לא אבלא). He mentions this past position again in v. 11b. חסד ואמת ('steadfast love and truth') are added to צדק. These three attributes are divine, given to man to be learned, pronounced and carried out.

37:6 - והוציא כאור צדקך He will cause your vindication to shine forth like a light,

ומשפטך כצהרים. the justice of your case, like the noonday sun.

58:2a - האמנם אלם צדק תדברון, [6] Oh mighty ones! Do you really proclaim just verdicts,

מישרים תשפטו? Do you judge with equity?

35:27 - ירנו וישמחו חפצי צדקי. May those who desire my vindication sing forth joyously.

His just acquittal by a just verdict will ensure him well being.

4:2a - בקראי ענני אלהי צדקי. Answer me when I call, the God of my vindication.

It is God who will ensure him his just verdict. Although צדק and תפילה do not exactly parallel one another, they are connected since both are audible terms. In 17:1 the psalmist says שמעה...צדק and here he says שמע תפילתי.

51:6 - למען-תצדק בדברך, So You are right when You proclaim Your vindication,

תזכה בשפטך. You are just when You judge.

I offer here a change in vocalization. Instead of בְּדָבְרֶךָ I read בְּדַבֶּרֶךָ, using the pi'el, and hence the reading: 'so You are right when You pronounce the just verdict.'[7]

Twice צדק ומשפט appear (89:15, 97:2) referring to God. Although they may be regarded as a fixed expression, like חכמה ודעת (Isa. 33:6),[8] for the totality of justice, there is a definite distinction between these two terms. When צדק precedes משפט, the moral aspect of what is right is emphasized.

צדק is a virtue, the quality, the ethical character of knowing what is proper and just. It is the ability to carry out this quality in public. When the king is said in

72:2 to judge במשפט וענייך בצדק עמך ('your people rightly, your lowly ones,

justly'), it becomes very clear: the king should judge his people with the quality

of צדק, according to the laws, e.g., those specified in Exod. 23:6-8, and Deut.

16:19.

The implementation of the law is through צדק. The idiom צדק ומשפט

encompasses the whole scope of justice: the ethics, the law and the process of the

judicial system. They dwell in God's abode: צדק ומשפט מכון כסא ('justice and

judgment are the base of His throne' – 97:2). They are the symbols of His

kingship.

צדקה', His overall divine ethics or attributes, is almost unanimously translated

by commentators as 'righteousness.'

When God will save His people, משפט will return to צדק and thus the balance

of justice will be restored (94:14-15).[9] Until then, the harmony in society is

wanting. צדק ומשפט emanate from God. They were given to mankind to be

implemented on earth. The same harmony and balance that exist in the divine

sphere are expected to be carried over to the human sphere.

35:24 - שפטני כצדקך! Judge me according to Your rightness!

The psalmist calls upon the divine attribute of justice to judge him. צדק is the

divine standard of what is right. He promises that when he is found innocent, he

will teach others these attributes. He will proclaim God's praises.[10]

The same meaning is found in 7:18, 35:28, 48:11, 50:6, 85:11-12,14, 97:6,

119:7,62,106,123,160,164.

119:75 - ידעתי כי-צדק משפטיך. I know, Adonai, that Your laws are just.

In v. 137 ישר replaces צדק: צדיק אתה ה' וישר משפטיך ('You are righteous,

Adonai, and Your judgments are upright'). Variations are found in v. 138: צדק

עדֹתֶיךָ ('Your just decrees'), and the same in v. 144 with a slight change in

vocalization: צֶדֶק עֵדְוֹתֶיךָ; v. 172: כל מצותיך צדק ('all Your laws are just'). The law is perceived as just. Similarly is שפט צדק in 9:5 ('a just judge').

45:5 - אמת-דבר-על רכב צלח   Ride triumphantly upon truth

וְעַנְוָה-צדק.   and just humility.

עות צדק is expected to be in a construct state as דבר-אמת. The noun is עֲוָה

and the form עֲוָה is odd and unique. It should either be עֲנָוָה or more likely

עֲנָוֹת, whereas עֲנָוֹת צדק will be 'proper humility,' although this expression is

unclear.

Dahood suggests an interesting reading, looking for imperative verbs: צְלַח,

רְכַב על דבר אמת וְעַנֵּה הַצְּדָּק ('Ride triumphantly in the cause of truth and

defend the poor'). This he bases on 82:3: עני ורש הצדיקו ('vindicate the lowly and

the poor').[11] Since we do not have here a legal connotation but a set of blessings

or general values of the king, this emendation is rejected.

It is clear that the text is difficult. I suggest a slight emendation by adding a

'ו' to צדק and thus to read: על דבר אמת, עֲנָוָה וצדק ('in the cause of truth,

humility, and justice'). In this way the psalmist blesses the king with three values

with which to serve his loving people. This I base on Zephaniah's words: בקשו צדק

בקשו עֲוָה ('pursue justice, pursue humility!' – 2:3).

The idea of wearing צדק (132:9) expresses a state in which the person attains

a special positive characteristic. He is clothed with an extra, exterior identity,

which is exposed to any observant. To wear צדק is a personal act, a free choice.

The wearer has dedicated himself to carry out the divine will.

In 132:16 God will dress His priests in salvation (ישע). Verse 9 relates to the

rightfulness of the Jerusalem priests in the cult, with no connection to justice.

Verse 16 refers to the perpetuity and legitimacy of David's dynasty in Zion.[12] The

priests stand against the dynasty's enemies of v. 18; salvation stands against

humiliation. Because of the eternity of David's dynasty and as a result of this

blessing—the eternity of Zion's priests—ישע is the eternal state of salvation in

which Zion, dynasty and priesthood will coexist. In this period of glory the priests will operate truthfully and rightly.

לבש צדק ('wear justice') and לבש ישע ('wear salvation') contrast with לבש בשת ('wear shame'). The main difference between לבש צדק and לבש ישע/בשת is that in the former case the person chooses voluntarily to be a just man (לבש is in pa'al), while in the latter case God inflicts salvation or shame on the person (לבש is in hif'il). The first two idioms are cause and effect: man chooses to be righteous, which results in God bringing about salvation to him.

צדק and ישע frequently appear as parallels in Deutero-Isaiah of the post-exilic period. Also, the idea of a perpetual Davidic dynasty is underscored from Jeremiah's time on. Both ideas of wearing ישע/צדק and the eternal Davidic House are found in Chronicles, which is also from a post-exilic era.[13] צדק and ישע originate in God and are given to the chosen ones, as רוח ה' ('the spirit of Adonai') is.[14]

Psalms uses צדק as an adverb in 9:9 (96:13, 96:9), 15:2, 17:15, 65:6, 72:2. The same usage appears in Prov. 8:8.[15] In 58:2 צדק can be read as an adverb, with a missing particle 'ב'. In 52:5 the psalmist accuses the false witness of loving שקר ('falsehood') and not testifying justly. Again we have דבר צדק, which may be a legal expression for the testimony of עד אמת ('a truthful witness'). According to v. 6 עד שקר ('a false witness') speaks דברי בלע ('pernicious words') or לשון מרמה ('treacherous speech'). However, צדק here may be another word for אמת, in opposition to צדק. Then צדק will be a noun, the direct object of דבר ('pronouncement'). At any rate, it seems that דבר שקר, דבר צדק, דבר בלע and מרמה לשון are all technical legal terms.

7:9 - שפטני ה', כצדקי.   Judge me, Adonai, according to my rightness.

This rightness is human. It is the reflection of God's righteousness on His follower. By keeping the divine laws, the devout keeps the ethical balance of society and this behavior is his צדק. This idea is clearly described in 18:21-25. It is summed up in v. 25a: וישב-ה' לי כצדקי ('and Adonai has requited me according to my rightness'). The same meaning is found in 45:8: אהבת צדק ותשׂנא רשׁע ('You love rightness and hate wickedness').

ROY A. ROSENBERG'S THEORY

1. THE GOD *ṢEDEQ*

The theory that there existed a god named *Ṣedeq* was promoted by Roy A. Rosenberg.[16] He argued that *Ṣedeq* was the local patron god of Jebusite Jerusalem, before its conquest by David. Later, this god is invoked as the patron of judgment (94:15).

Rosenberg bases his theory on a number of factors, among them the names of the king-priests of Jerusalem: Malki-Ṣedeq (Gen. 14) and Adoni-Ṣedeq (Josh. 10). To these names he adds the names of Zadok, who appears with no genealogy, as one of David's military commanders (1 Chron. 12:28).

Harold H. Rowley suggested in 1939 that the root *ṣdq* is characteristic of Jebusites in Jerusalem.[17] Christian H. Hauer agrees with Rowley saying that any name bearing the root *ṣdq* in the Davidic period would be Jerusalem born.[18] However, many scholars, including Rosenberg,[19] showed that names with the element *ṣdq* were common among all Semitic societies, e.g., Ugaritic (Ṣdq'il, Ṣdqšlm), Amorite (Ammiṣaduqa), South Arabian (Ilṣaduq), Canaanite of the Amarna letters (Rabṣidqi) and Hebrew (Ṣidqiya).

Rosenberg asserts that once the Jerusalem cult was established in the monarchy, the attributes of the god *Ṣedeq* as the god of justice, righteousness and propriety, were applied to Adonai. *Ṣedeq* of Adonai is the characteristic of the god *Ṣedeq*, that became part of the body of Adonai.[20] His examples are from Ps. 48:11: צדק מלאה ימינך ('*Ṣedeq* fills Your right hand'),[21] and Isa. 41:10: אף-תמכתיך בימין צדקי ('I have upheld you בימין צדקי'). This צדק or right hand/arm of God, is the part of Him which performs all the glorious, victorious acts.[22]

Rosenberg contradicts himself. Earlier in the article he says that *Ṣedeq* was the sun-god whose attribute was justice. Later he states that the *Ṣedeq* of Adonai in Deutero-Isaiah and in some psalms characterized God's acts of salvation and victories. These attributes or characteristics are not the same.

Rosenberg adduces more evidence for his theory. *Ṣedeq*, he asserts, was also part of God's divine court, as expressed in Ps. 89:15: צדק ומשפט מכון כסאך.[22] In 85:14 צדק לפניו יהלך is to be accepted literally, namely, '*Ṣedeq* walks before Him.' In vv. 11-12 '*Ṣedeq* and *Shalom* (manifestation of the god *Šalem*) kiss one another, *Emet* (manifestation of the god *Amin*) springs forth from the earth, while *Ṣedeq* looks down from heaven.'[23]

Rosenberg goes too far when he attributes to Isaiah the belief that Jerusalem was the city where *Ṣedeq* dwells (צדק ילין בה – Isa. 1:21,26).[25] He ignores the parallelism of משפט and צדק, unless he regards משפט as a manifestation of a god too.[26] He also claims that Jeremiah acknowledged that Jerusalem was 'the habitation of *Ṣedeq*' (31:22)[27] when the prophet called the Temple Mount נוה צדק. The connection of *Ṣedeq* to the Temple is strengthened by the psalmist, in 118:19, who calls the Temple gates שערי-צדק ('the gates of *Ṣedeq*').[28]

Rosenberg sees a continuous struggle among the kings either to establish or to destroy the "legitimate Jerusalemite sun cult." The religious representatives in Jerusalem were also divided on this issue. Isaiah, for one, advocated the legitimacy of *Ṣedeq*. The Deuteronomist integrated *Ṣedeq*'s attributes into the oneness of Adonai. That was when *Ṣedeq*, the 'arm' and 'right hand' of Adonai, became part of the theology of Adonai.

Whitley rejects Rosenberg's idea because, he says, Deutero-Isaiah could not have accepted the existence of a foreign deity alongside Adonai. *Ṣedeq*, the god, became part of Adonai in the same way as Adonai adopted the powers of Baal and Anat as deities who defeated Tehom, Tanin and Mut. צדק, according to Deutero-Isaiah, meant the *power* and *being* of Adonai.[29]

Rosenberg's theory is utterly rejected. In 85:11-14 four divine attributes are mentioned: חסד, אמת, צדק and שלום. These attributes are bestowed, this time, on nature to bring rain so that the land will yield its produce. צדק walks before Adonai so as to clear the way and to announce His presence. That kindness, truth, "righteousness" and peace meet and kiss is merely a metaphor. The author uses more metaphors in vv. 12 and 14 which may reflect Canaanite myths. If צדק was conceived as a god then חסד, אמת and שלום should be regarded as gods too.

Also, why do we not hear of psalms written to the god Ṣedeq or any other acknowledgment of his existence? The imagery of walking before God is common, e.g. Ps. 86:11, 89:16, 56:14, Gen. 24:40, 48:15, Prov. 8:20. Only Adonai walks on wings of wind (Ps. 104:3). Even the description of Habakkuk (3:5,11) of דבר ('pestilence'), רשף ('flames of fire'), שמש ('sun') and ירח ('moon'), though said to walk before God, lack the divinity of these Canaanite gods.[30] They are conceived by Habakkuk as the means by which God punishes Israel's enemies: by disease, fire and changes in nature. This imagery of walking before God refers to behavior which is in accord with His will. If these four concepts were gods then זעם ('rage') and אף ('fury') in v. 12 should be considered as such.

This discussion is not about challenges to Canaanite mythology, nor about the means of punishment that God takes, but about positive attributes of God. Just as חסד, אמת and משפט are attributes, צדק belongs to this category as well. No other positive attribute of God has been considered by scholars to be a god. Similar are the attributes of הוד והדר ('glory and majesty'), עז ותפארת ('Strength and splendor') mentioned in Ps. 96:6.

The same consideration applies to כי עד-צדק ישוב משפט ואחריו כל-ישרי-לב in 94:1 and to אז תחפץ זבחי-צדק in 51:21. The psalmist believes that when the law is restored to its proper place (עד may mean 'throne' as 'd in Ugaritic literature UT 127:22-24),[31] then all upright hearts will follow it.

2. זבחי צדק

51:21 - אז תחפץ זבחי-צדק   Then You will want the right sacrifices,

עלה וכליל.   burnt and whole offerings.

In vv. 18-20 the psalmist feels that at this time of national destruction God does not wish for sacrifices. Only after the rebuilding of Zion will He welcome proper sacrifices—זבחי צדק.

Moses Buttenweiser translates: 'sacrifices for righteousness' sake,' explaining that צדק is the righteous living that demands sacrifices. He says that "צדק is qualificative genitive," in the like of כלי מות ('death-bearing weapons' – Ps. 7:14).[32] That is, make sacrifices that will bring about righteousness. This ex-planation is nebulous. Do sacrifices cause or bring righteousness? The idea is odd since the call to repent does not demand sacrifices but a change of heart.

Dahood translates 'legitimate'[33] while Roger O'Callaghan reads 'lawful (or legitimate) sacrifices.' He bases this reading on KRT, lines 12-13.[34]

The word זבח refers to the type of sacrifice or celebration by a group of people, with no mention of a god's name anywhere: זבח פסח ('the Passover sacrifice' – Exod. 12:27), זבח שלמים ('a sacrifice of well-being' or 'peace offering' – Lev. 3:1), זבח תודה ('a thanksgiving sacrifice' – Lev. 7:13), זבח נדר ('a votive offering'), זבח נדבה ('a freewill offering'), both in Lev. 7:16, זבח הימים ('the annual offering' – 1 Sam. 1:21), זבח משפחה ('a family feast' – 1 Sam. 20:29), זבח העם ('the people's sacrifice' – Ez. 46:24), זבח תרועה ('an offering with a shout of joy' – Ps. 27:6).

It can be the type of animal to be sacrificed: זבח הבקר ('sacrifices of oxen' – 2 Chron. 7:5); or it can describe the type of people who sacrifice: זבח רשעים ('the sacrifice of the wicked' – Prov. 21:27).

In 1:8 Zephaniah describes allegorically the Day of Punishment as יום זבח ה' ('the day of Adonai's sacrifice').

The psalmist of 51:21 explicitly mentions זבחי צדק as a type of sacrifice, when he mentions them together with "holocaust and whole offering." It is very clear that זבחי צדק have nothing to do with a god 'Ṣedeq.'

וזבח אלהים (51:19) is probably an error. אלהים is erroneously repeated from the end of the verse, and should be omitted. The psalmist says that since God is not interested in sacrifices, all he can give Him is sacrifices of his broken spirit and heart. This, he hopes, God will not reject.

The psalmist of 4:6 asks the sinners to sacrifice just and proper sacrifices and to trust Him. The idea of calling the people to sacrifice for a Canaanite deity, so that they will be helped by Adonai, is far-fetched and baseless. Even if one believes that צדק is a survival of a local deity adapted by the Israelites at an early stage of their settlement in Canaan, or projected upon Adonai, his initial significance and function had long disappeared from the Israelite culture, the Temple rituals and hymns. The Scriptures do not support such forced and alien ideas.

At a period when prophets and priests of Judah called for cleansing the religion, the tradition and the customs of any foreign influence, it is inconceivable and groudless to suggest that they accepted the existence of a Canaanite god along-side Adonai.

In זבחו זבחי צדק (4:6) Targum does not see sacrifices but an allegory for self-restraint which will be considered by God to be righteousness. Similarly, Ibn Ezra as well as Rashi do not see actual sacrifices but an allegory for doing righteous acts.[35]

Snaith, following his understanding of the word צדק, explains that these are sacrifices which conform to the regulations, like אבני צדק.[36]

In Deut. 33:19 the expression זבחי צדק appears in poetry:

עמים הר יקראו

שם יזבחו זבחי-צדק.

I suggest to read יִקָּרְאוּ (in nif'al) instead of the Massorah יִקְרָאוּ (in pa'al) and the meaning will be; 'Nations will be summoned[37] on a mountain, where they will offer the right sacrifices,' as the law and custom require. The custom of sacrificing on mountains was common.[38]

Driver reads: 'They call people to (the) mountain, there they offer sacrifices of righteousness.' He explains זבחי-צדק as "sacrifices offered in a right frame of mind, the outcome of a right spirit."[39]

3. מלכי-צדק (Malki-Ṣedeq)[40]

111:4b - עַל-דִּבְרָתִי מַלְכִּי-צֶדֶק

Assumingly, this is a difficult verse. God vows that David will be a priest forever. God will stand by his right side to eliminate his enemies. Dahood recognizes a third person singular -y in דברתי and מלכי which refers to God.[41]

These four words may be read in various ways: as part of God's oath, or as the psalmist's words. Then על-דברתי can be read 'on my word,' 'on His word,' 'according to His words' (if we accept the third person singular reading), or the like.

Another suggestion is to omit the suffix 'י' of דברתי and either leave or omit the suffix 'י' of מלכי—צדק-(י)מלכ(י)—על-דברת(י)—and consequently translate, after Eccles. 3:18, 7:14, 'for a (my) just king;' or after Dan. 2:30, 4:14, 'so that a (my) just king (will be established);' or after Eccles. 8:2, 'concerning a (my) just king.'[42]

Buttenwieser translates: 'after the manner of Melchiṣedek.' He explains that since it is a post-exilic, messianic psalm, the psalmist promises the Messiah-to-come both functions that the original Malki-Ṣedeq held: priesthood and king-ship.[43]

One interpretation is as follows: God announces that His king will serve Him faithfully, and will be a righteous or rightful king. Perhaps in the post-exilic Messianic theology מלכי-צדק became a symbol for the legitimate king to come. The proper name became an epithet for the Messiah. Support for this assumption is found in a Pesher from Qumran, cave 11. There, Malki-Ṣedeq is mentioned as a heavenly redemption figure who will appear in the Jubilee Year as God's messenger to execute the divine judgment at the end of days.[44]

I offer a new reading of the text based on a Biblical literary style: The idea that originally Ps. 110:4 talks about the king Malki-Ṣedeq of Gen. 14 has no basis at all. The addition of a yohd in דברתי and מלכי is not more than a poetic form (litterae compaginis) chosen by the psalmist, like לחושבי, מקימי, המשפילי, המגביהי, and מושבי (Ps. 113:5-9).[45] There is no reason to find here a third person singular form. על-דברתי is a poetic form for the prosaic על-דְּבָר.[46] In 79:9 the poet uses על-דבר which has the same meaning as על-דברתי of 110:4.

מלכי-צדק of Psalms 110 is similar to Jeremiah's צמח צדקה (33:15), the ethical king in whose time God will bring peace to Israel.

The only commentator who comes closest to the true meaning of the verse is Ibn Ezra, who senses the incongruity of על-דברתי with מלכי-צדק and sees no reference to 'word.' He reads על-דברתי as if it was written על-דבר ('for') and explains בעבור שאתה מלך צדק 'for you are a righteous king.'[47]

One more point has to be mentioned, which concerns Zadoq. Following the conclusions of Frank Cross and Menahem Haran,[48] Saul Olyan rejects the Jebusite theory. He methodically proves that Zadoq was not a Jebusite priest but belonged to an Aaronid family that settled in Qabṣeel in the southern part of Judah.[49]

John Gammie, too, does not see any original connection between Zadoq and Malki-Ṣedeq of Šalem. If Zadoq was a Jebusite priest in Jerusalem, he (or his supporters) took the Malki-Ṣedek tradition from Shechem, which moved later to Shiloh and then to Nov. From there they established the legitimacy of Zadoq's priestly family in the Israelite religion.[50]

With this, all the points scholars have raised to prove the theory of the god Ṣedeq, have been refuted.

Let us continue now with the examination of צדק in Psalms.

שערי-צדק - 118:19   The gates of the rightness

These are gates through which only the righteous (צדיקם) can pass (v. 20).

The description of the gates reflects on the people who use them.[51]

Buttenwieser dismisses the interpretation of 'gates' and considers them as an allegory for the prophetic idea that "righteousness is the bond that can bring man close to God."[52]

Targum, Rashi and others explain שערי-צדק as either the gates of Jerusalem, which are named צדק (after Isa. 1:26), or as the gates of the Temple, after the idea that only the righteous will pass through them.

מעגלי-צדק - 23:3   The right paths

מעגל, which parallels ארח (17:4,5), דרך and נתיב (Isa. 59:8), they all mean a 'way,' 'path.'[53] In all passages the psalmist declares that he walks in the way of God. This way leads to green meadows and tranquil waters. These are the right ways of God (מעגלי-צדק). The idea that the paths of God lead to righteousness is possible but not necessary.[54]

From all the passages quoted we can see that מעגלי-צדק means the right ways which the devout chooses in order to acquire peace (מי מנחות—tranquil waters), goodness (טוב) and kindness (חסד). This צדק is divine in origin. Wisdom uses מעגלי ישר ('upright paths') which are synonymous with דרך חכמה—the path of Wisdom (Prov.4:11). The idea is the same: one chooses the paths of Wisdom, the other—the paths of what is right according to God's teaching. The psalmist trusts the just ways of God without explaining their nature.

2. PROVERBS

שפתי-צדק - 16:13   The lips of rightness (the just lips)

The right words are the proper, honest words that the lips of the righteous utter.[55] They please kings. Kings love those who speak honestly (דֹּבֵר יְשָׁרִים). One can read דָּבָר for דֹּבֵר to parallel with שׂפה (tongue, speech) but not necessarily.[56] דֹּבֵר יְשָׁרִים equate with שׂפתי-צדק as singular and plural usages are exchanged for poetic style. צדק is what is straight and honest.

A very similar proverb appears in 10:32: שׂפתי צדיק ידעו רצון ('The lips of the righteous know what is pleasing'). שפתי-צדק are those of צדיק שפתי, who bring

pleasure to the listener.

25:5 - הגו רשע לפני-מלך   Remove the wicked from the king's presence

ויכן בצדק כסאו.   and his throne will be rightly established.

By removing impurities from silver, the silversmith makes a proper vessel (v.

4); so is the case with the wicked. When he is removed from the king's presence,

the throne is properly, honestly founded. Getting rid of negative influences results

in establishing what is right and pure. Consequently, such a throne (or a vessel)

endures longer and functions better.[57]

1:3 (2:9) - צדק ומשפט ומישרים.   rightness and justice and equity.

As mentioned above, when צדק precedes משפט it emphasizes the ethical aspect

of law in court. משפט stands for the legal aspect, while מישרים is either a general

term for what is right or it is connected with the function of the king as keeper of

the law.[58] By learning and understanding Wisdom (1:2, 2:2-4), one will eventually

comprehend the knowledge of God (2:5), which leads to צדק ומשפט ומישרים כל מעגל

טוב ('rightness, justice and equity—every good course').

Wisdom is the means by which one acquires divine attributes. צדק has become

the goal. Effective and dedicated learning will result in צדק. The knowledge of

God protects the wise from evil and twisted ways (2:11-12,16, 3:25). It prolongs

life and makes it enjoyable and satisfying (3:2,4,10,12,16-18). Wisdom literature

is concerned with the ethical aspect of life (צדק) rather than with its legal view

(משפט).

According to William McKane, words like צדק, משפט and מישרים "contrast

strongly with the original lack of moral commitment in the vocabulary of old

Wisdom."[59] That is, צדק in old wisdom did not carry any moral aspect. The moral

aspect was reinterpreted by the prophets. In 2:9 he explains what צדק is. He

translates: "Then you will discern what is right and just and straight." "Right-

eousness," he says, "is the state of the man who walks in Yahweh's ways."[60] Thus,

Wisdom is the means, צדק is the state of being, and the end result is harmony between God and man. Then the wise becomes a צדיק.

8:15-16 - בי מלכים ימלכו   Through me kings reign

ורזנים יחקק צדק;   and rulers decree just laws;

בי שרים ישרו   Through me princes rule,

ונדיבים כל-שפטי ארץ.   great men and all the judges of the land.

Wisdom is the tool with which the leaders administer the law. However, v. 15b seems to be missing the word חוק or משפט. It should have been יחקקו חוק צדק ('they will legislate right laws') or יחקקו משפט צדק as Ibn Ezra suggests. The connection between צדק, שפטים and מלכים is clear. The word יחקק ('will legislate') makes it even clearer.

McKane translates: 'rulers enact what is right,'[61] while Robert Scott translates: 'make just decrees.'[62] Crawford Toy translates: 'administer justice.'[63]

כל-שפטי ארץ sums up the leaders who deal with legislation. The law enacted is right, since it was conceived by Wisdom. In some texts צדק appears instead of ארץ (see Mikraot Gedolot). The expression יחקקו צדק has no parallel (ימלכו parallels ישרו). We would expect ונדיבים ישפטו ('great men will judge') or ושפטים ישפטו ('and judges will judge').

31:9 - פתח-פיך, שפט-צדק   Speak up, judge justly

ודין עני ואביון!   and judge the poor and the needy!

Again, we have the legal aspect of צדק that parallels דין (also vv. 5,8b). The duty of King Lemuel is here drawn. Sobriety enables the king to judge his people justly. One does not judge 'justice' but 'justly.'

Commentators translate here loosely: 'pronounce thy judgments with equity;'[64] 'Speak out to ensure that justice is done;'[65] 'Speak out! See justice done.'[66]

12:17 - יפיח אמונה יגיד צדק,   He who testifies truthfully tells right testimony,

ועד שקרים מרמה.   but a false witness (tells) deceit.

The legal aspect of צדק is clear. שפתי-שקר ('lying speech'—v. 22a), עד שקרים

('a false witness'—v. 17), and לשׁון שׁקר ('a lying tongue'—v.19b) stand against יגיד

צדק ('he will utter what is right') and שׂפת אמת ('truthful speech') both in v. 19a.

Other legal terms are: דבר-שׁקר ('a lie' - 13:5a), עד אמונים ('an honest witness'

- 14:5a), עד שׁקר ('a false witness' - 14:5b), שׂפתי-צדק ('truthful speech' - 16:13).

All deal with utterance of testimony in court. The act of proclaiming the right and

true evidence brings forth innocence, and thus—justice. McKane reads יָפִיחַ for

יָפִיחַ and parallels it with עד which is unnecessary, since יפיח and יגיד are both

in the same tense and in the third person. This change he bases on the Ugaritic text

no. 57: yph kn'm.

The verb יפיח applies to מרמה in the second colon. יגיד צדק is the opposite of

יפיח מרמה, thus צדק means 'truth' which shares the meaning of אמונה.

3. JOB

31:6 - ישׁקלני במאזני-צדק   Let Him weigh me on a right/just scale

וידע אלוה תמתי.   and let God ascertain my innocence.

צדק and תֻמָּה are the opposites of שׁוא ('falsehood') and מרמה ('deceit') of

v. 5, namely, they convey the meaning of truth, innocence and perfection. The

scales will show that, if weighed, Job will be found full weight. מאזני צדק is the

commercial term for 'right scales,' which includes איפת צדק, הין צדק and אבן צדק.

The opposite is מאזני מרמה found in Hos. 12:8 and Prov. 11:1.

6:29 - שׁבו נא, אל-תהי עולה   Relent, let there not be injustice,

ושׁבו, עוד צדקי-בה.   relent, I am still in the right.

עולה[67] ('wrong') is the opposite of צדק ('right'). It is reiterated in v. 30, where

עולה and הוות ('falsehood') are mentioned as vices that Job's mouth lacks. צדק

is his overall righteousness, his innocence and integrity, as against עולה which

denotes the general wrongfulness, either in doing, thinking and more so—in

uttering.

8:6 - אם-זך וישׁר אתה   If you are pure and upright

כי-עתה יעיר עליך   He will surely protect you

ושלם מזת-צדקך.   and grant well-being to your righteous home.

מזת-צדקך[68] bears the same form as משפטי צדקך ('Your just laws' - Ps. 119:106), מעון קדשך ('Your holy abode' - Deut. 26:15), and נזה קדשך ('Your holy abode' - Exod. 15:13). Jeremiah calls the Temple Mount נוה צדק (31:22) as well as God (50:7). Proverbs repeats this expression twice in נוה צדיקים (3:33) and נוה צדיק (24:15).

Bildad talks about God as the keeper of משפט and צדק (8:3). These attributes are His criteria for justice in society (vv. 4-7,20-22) and in nature (vv. 9-12). If Job is upright so is his house.[69] The opposite of נוה צדק, according to Bildad, is אהל רשעים ('the tent of the wicked' - v. 22), which falls for lack of divine protection.

הזאת חשבת למשפט - 35:2   Do you think it just

אמרת צדקי מאל?   to say, "my rightness is more than God's"?

The LXX, Peshita, Targum and Vulgate read: צדקתי - 'I am more right(eous) than God.' Most commentators concur with this reading.

The word צדק serves both v. 2 and v. 3. However, this idea does not preclude God's righteousness. Job acknowledges God's righteousness, but at the same time he asserts his own. This צדק is the human right behavior as we have seen in Ps. 7:9 and 18:25. Elihu cannot find compatibility here. What he concludes is that Job puts his rightness above God's and by so doing he denies God's righteousness. This was the reason for Elihu to storm into the debate.

האל יעות משפט, - 8:3   Will God pervert justice,

ואם-שדי יעות-צדק?   will the Almighty pervert rightness?

צדק can be understood in two ways:

1. Would God distort what is right, His rightness?

2. Would God distort a just verdict?

In both cases צדק is a judicial term. In 34:12 לא-יעות משפט parallels לא ירשיע, meaning, God will not distort judgment, nor will declare a false verdict.

36:3 - ‏אשא דעי למרחוק,‏   I will make my opinion widely known,

‏ולפעלי אתן-צדק.‏   I will justify my action.

Elihu says that his actions, as his words, are justifiable.

4. QOHELETH

3:16 - ‏מקום המשפט שמה הרשע,‏   At the place of justice there is wickedness,

‏ומקום הצדק שמה הרשע.‏   and at the place of rightness there is wickedness.

5:7 - ‏אם עשק רש וגזל משפט וצדק‏   If you see in the state oppression of the poor and

‏תראה במדינה...‏   suppression of justice and rightness...

7:15 - ‏יש צדיק אבד בצדקו,‏   Sometime a righteous man perishes in spite of his

rightness,

‏ויש רשע מאריך ברעתו.‏   and sometimes a wicked man endures in spite of his

wickedness.

‏רשע‏, a general term for evil, is in contrast to ‏משפט‏, a general term for justice. ‏צדק‏ parallels ‏משפט‏ and they both relate to justice in court. ‏משפט וצדק‏ ('justice') is an expression that contrasts ‏עשק‏ and ‏גזל‏ ('injustice'). Their legal association is enhanced by the word ‏במדינה‏ ('in the state', 'in the government', 'in the judicial system'). ‏משפט‏ refers more specifically to the fixed, permanent laws, while ‏צדק‏ is its implementation. The expression ‏משפט וצדק‏ emphasizes the legal aspect of justice, associated with authority. In all cases ‏צדק‏ is what is right, the rightness of man.

Scott reads ‏צדיק‏ for ‏צדק‏ and ‏רָשָׁע‏ for ‏רֶשַׁע‏. He bases his emendation on the LXX and Targum. This avoids the repetition in the second colon, but it is not necessary. In 5:7 he translates 'right'[70] for ‏צדק‏ and in 7:15—'innocence.'[71]

‏צדק‏ is translated by A. Lukyn Williams as 'righteousness'. He explains it as "the quality that moves him to give a right judgment." To avoid repetition he suggests reading ‏פֶּשַׁע‏ ('transgression') for ‏רֶשַׁע‏ as others do.[72]

It is interesting to note that Sforno explains ‏צדק‏ of 3:16 as 'righteous verdicts.'[73]

Ibn Ezra explains בצדק as the person who misunderstands 'being righteous' as doing the extreme, such as bringing constant afflictions upon himself. Rashi explains differently: although he is suffering, he still adheres to his righteousness.[74]

At the basis of 7:15 lies the belief that צדק is associated with long life. Proverbs associates longevity with the knowledge of God and Wisdom (9:11, 10:2). The connection is apparent since צדק and חכמה are the creations of God. The צדיק is the wise man.[75]

Summary: In Psalms, צדק has various meanings, depending upon its associative range. It also refers to either man or God.

It comes with verbs that indicate audibility, e.g. בשר ('proclaim'), דבר ('speak'), הגה ('utter'), ידה ('confess'), הגד ('say') and שמע ('hear/tell'). צדק is heard in court, which can mean giving evidence, explaining the case or announcing a just verdict. It can also simply mean 'truth.'

Within this social, legal sphere, צדק is probably a legal term for speaking the truth in court.

צדק also is symbolized by light, which stands for purity and rightness.

The judge, who carries his duty properly, is said to wear צדק. He is endowed with the attribute of justice. לבש צדק alternates with לבש ישע, and contrasts with לבש בשת. The cause (צדק) and effect (ישע) are indicative of behavior and divine reward. However, with the influence of Wisdom on some psalmists, this reward is depicted as a state of rest, peace, goodness and kindness. This development in meaning could be achieved because צדק bears also a divine connotation. The state of peaceful existence is compared to נאות דשא ('pastures') and to מי מנחות ('restful waters'). Its opposition is גיא צלמות ('the valley of the shadow of death,' or 'the dark valley').

צדק is associated with the attribute of humility, with court setting (משפט, מישרים, אמת, שקר) and with peace. Its opposite is רשע ('wickedness').

Within the religious sphere, when צדק is connected with verbs of hearing, it parallels תהלות, God's wondrous deeds. Here, too, צדק is associated with שפט: it is the criterion by which God judges man. This attribute creates good laws. Their revelation among men brings about salvation. They are eternal.

צדק is symbolized by the hand (arm) of God, to illustrate His awesome power.

When צדק ומשפט refer to God, they mean the totality of His attribute of justice. They symbolize His kingship. They are the absolute and ultimate criterion of justice.

When the leader (king or judge) does צדק he follows the divine criterion and thus secures peace not only between man and his fellow man, but also between man and God. צדק is a term within the religious and secular spheres.

צדק is used as an adverb and as an adjective.

In Proverbs, as in Psalms, the meanings of צדק vary. Only in the legal aspect is its meaning clear. It is what is just and correct in accordance with the law. It is associated with שפט, דין and with giving testimony. Uttering צדק is speaking honestly.

While Psalms uses דבר צדק, that which עד אמת pronounces, here we have הגד צדק, which stands in opposition to עד שקרים.

As in Psalms צדק is strongly associated with kingship. The throne is secured by establishing justice.

Outside its legal connotation, the meaning of צדק is not clear-cut. It fluctuates between the intellectual activity of man (learning Wisdom which is equated with the knowledge of God) and the goal itself. It is also the ethical aspect of life. צדק, משפט and מישרים are elements or components in what Wisdom calls 'the good path.'

In Job צדק is the human innocence and integrity, which is projected on his home (נוה צדק). It is associated with other terms that indicate innocence: זך ('pure,' 'immaculate'), ישר ('upright'), תמה ('innocence') and משפט ('judgment,' 'law') in a court setting. צדק and משפט are juristic terms. The reward for being righteous

is divine protection. צדק is the opposite of שׁוא, הוח ('falsehood'), מרמה ('deceit')
and עולה ('wrong').

When צדק refers to God it parallels משׁפט. Divine justice, the way it is
understood by Job and his friends, is a direct and just connection between sin and
punishment, right and reward. They see צדק and משׁפט of God in terms of a human
juristic system.[76] צדק, then, is the divine criterion for justice, as portrayed in
Psalms.

צדק in Qoheleth is a legal term (3:16, 5:7). It is associated with משׁפט
('litigation', 'justice system'). Then it is probably the executive aspect of court
procedures which carries the idea of justice done. It is the beacon of justice of the
authorities. Its opposites are רשׁע ('wickedness'), עשׁק ('oppression') and גזל
('robbery').

צדק is also the attribute of the righteous, which contrasts with רעה ('wrong
ways') of the wicked. Both terms delineate the overall good/bad character of a
person.

TABLE 4

Book	Judicial System: plea, right, verdict, vindication, testimony, executive branch	Rightness of man	Rightness of king
Ps.	10	5	2
Prov.	1	2	3
Job	1	2	-
Qoh.	2	3	-

(Table 4 continued)

Book	Rightness of God	Right, true, just, proper	Rightly, truly, justly	Truth
Ps.	19	13	7	1
Prov.	-	1	-	-
Job	1	2	-	2
Qoh.	-	-	-	-

6

צְדָקָה
IN THE WISDOM LITERATURE

THE BLESSED LIFE

PSALM

5:9 - ...ה', נְחֵנִי בְצִדְקָתֶךָ   Adonai, lead me with Your righteousness...

הַיְשַׁר לְפָנַי דַרְכֶּךָ.   make Your way straight before me.

צְדָקָה is the Way of God which is straight. Guidance in life is needed because of those lying in wait, the insidious foes. This צְדָקָה blesses the supplicant (v. 13), keeps him happy and protected (v.12). It is a moral protection, rather than physical.[1]

The reading should be דַרְכִּי ('my path') instead of דַרְכֶּךָ ('Your path'), since the poet is praying for a straight path to walk on, to prevent him from falling.[2] There is no question or doubt in the believer's mind that God's path is straight and it does not require straightening. Only by taking the right path and being a blameless person, can he be justified in calling for God's judgment on his adversaries. The change from first person to third person was probably done in order to rhyme with בְּצִדְקָתֶךָ.

Franciscus Zorell defines צְדָקָה as divine 'generous gifts' as found in 72:3.[3] Based on this interpretation, Dahood translates צְדָקָה in 24:5 as 'generous treatment.'[4]

The request to be led in God's path is 'for the sake of' (לְמַעַן) God's name (23:3, 31:4, 143:10b-11a). The poet asks God in 27:11 to lead him on His straight path—אֹרַח מִישׁוֹר—that leads to life in the 'land of life,' where His goodness resides (v. 13).[5]

143:8-12 - In v. 10b אֶרֶץ מִישׁוֹר ('flat land,' 'level ground') is associated with life: the straight land is the path that the poet wants to find (v. 8). אֶרֶץ and דֶּרֶךְ interchange.

The structure, style and ideas in vv. 8-12 are as follows:

(4) - ...הוֹדִיעֵנִי דֶּרֶךְ-זוּ אֵלֵךְ   Let me know the road I must take...

(3) - תַּנְחֵנִי בְּאֶרֶץ מִישׁוֹר,   lead me on a flat/straight land,

(4) - !לְמַעַן שִׁמְךָ, ה', תְּחַיֵּנִי   For the sake of Your name, O Adonai, preserve me!

(4) - בְּצִדְקָתְךָ תּוֹצִיא מִצָּרָה נַפְשִׁי,   In Your righteousness free me from distress,

(3) - !וּבְחַסְדְּךָ תַּצְמִית אֹיְבָי   In Your love/kindness put an end to my foes!

(4) - וְהַאֲבַדְתָּ כָּל-צֹרְרֵי נַפְשִׁי   Destroy all my mortal enemies

(3) - .כִּי אֲנִי עַבְדֶּךָ   for I am Your servant.

The poet plays on words and sounds. The sound of 'צ' is repeated several times in verses 8-12 for sound effect: מִצָּרָה, תּוֹצִיא, בְּצִדְקָתְךָ, בְּאֶרֶץ, רְצוֹנֶךָ, הַצִּילֵנִי, תַּצְמִית, and צֹרְרֵי. Throughout the same verses the sound 'e' is generously used: כִּי, תַּצְמִית, תּוֹצִיא, תְּחֵנִי, תְּחֵנִי, לְמַדֵּנִי, בַּסִּיתִי, הַצִּילֵנִי, נֶפֶשׁ (3), נָשָׂאתִי, הוֹדִיעֵנִי, בָטַחְתִּי and אֲנִי.

He intentionally uses the similarly-sound words תַּנְחֵנִי and תְּחַיֵּנִי at the beginning and at the end of a verse (10b-11a).

By living in the 'straight land' the poet survives his troubles. This land/path endows life. צדקה and חסד are God's messengers to lead him out of his misery. In 43:3 אוֹר ('light') and אֱמֶת ('truth') are two other messengers to lead him to the tranquility and safety of God's dwelling.

68:28 - תְּנָה-עָוֺן עַל-עֲוֺנָם   Add sin upon their iniquities

!וְאַל-יָבֹאוּ בְּצִדְקָתֶךָ   let them have no share in Your Blessed Life!

צדקה is again associated with life. It is the land of life that the righteous are entitled to enter, having been inscribed in the book of life.

119:40 - הנה תאבתי לפקדיך   See, I have longed for Your precepts,

בצדקתך חיני!   In Your righteousness preserve me!

In v. 37 the poet says בדרכך חיני and in v. 88—חיני כחסדך. The divine צדקה, חדך and חסד grant life. Living in ארח/ארץ מישור assures the psalmist of blessing, peace, abundance and longevity. This "righteousness," as I have translated, encompasses an aggregate of ideas and beliefs of a *full, blessed and protected life* in a divine location somewhere on this earth. In this life there is no physical or emotional pain; no impediments or adversaries.

Metaphorically, life is compared to a straight, flat land that has no crooked paths on which to stumble. If this life is the salvific idea that was crystallized in the post-exilic era, then one can translate this צדקה as ישועה/תשועה/ישע. However, this salvation that the psalmists call for is here on earth, and not in the world to come. Their immediate need for help is very real.

This life is very ideal, though, since the divine צדקה cannot be completely transferred to mankind. It can be partially achieved and that will suffice too. It is easy to understand why commentators like Ibn Ezra, Briggs and Dahood find this צדקה in heaven.

88:13 - היודע בחשך פלאך   Are Your wonders made known in the netherworld

וצדקתך בארץ נשיה?   and Your Blessed Life in the land of oblivion?

The poet wants God to make that blessed life known now, here, and not in the land of the dead (vv. 12-13). פלא, אמונה, חסד and צדקה are the ingredients that this צדקה/life consists of.[6] In v. 11 צדקה is in contrast to מתים ('the dead'), רפאים ('the shades'), in v. 12 it contrasts קבר ('grave') and אבדון ('place of perdition'), and in v. 13—חשך and ארץ נשיה. These are synonyms for the netherworld.[7]

143:1 - באמנתך עני,   Answer me by Your truth,

בצדקתך!   (answer me) by Your righteousness!

The poet calls on God to save him by way of His אמונה and צדקה. He used to live in that blessed life (v. 4a) but somehow he was dragged into the darkness, into the netherworld (v. 3). From this depression he calls God to show him the path back to the blessed life (vv. 8b,11-12a). With His good spirit God will lead him to safety (v. 10).

וחסד ה' מעולם ועד-עולם על-יראיו, - 103:17   But Adonai's steadfast love is for all

eternity toward those who fear Him,

וצדקתו לבני בנים.   and His righteousness is for the children's children.

The psalmist asserts that the divine חסד and צדקה are there forever to be granted to the righteous people. This blessed life stands in contrast to the temporary life of man (vv. 15-16). According to vv. 4b-5a God renews life with His חסד ('love'), רחמים ('mercy') and טוב ('goodness').

In Wisdom psalm 112 instead of חסד we find ברכה ('blessing') through the its verb יברך ('will be blessed' – v. 2), הון-ועשר ('wealth and riches' – v. 3) and כבוד ('honor' – v. 9), which are the divine gifts given to the righteous. God has a sense of Justice (v. 5), he gives lavishly to the needy (v. 9). צדקה, then, is a state of living the good life that is obtained through good deeds. Job expressed that well without employing the word צדקה (ch. 29).

Amos Ḥakham offers two interpretations: צדקה is 'right,' or a collective noun for all righteous people, like כהונה ('priesthood') in the Rabbinic literature, to denote all priests.[8] He probably follows Targum which translates 'and let them not have the right to enter where the righteous gather.' Targum alludes to a place, which corresponds with my interpretation.

צדקה and life are associated also in Proverbs:

PROVERBS

רדף צדקה וחסד - 21:21   He who strives to do good and kind deeds

ימצא חיים צדקה וכבוד.   attains life, blessing and honor.

The double meaning of צדקה is clearly described here. Through good deeds one acquires that state of blessed life, peace and contentment.[9] It comes instead of 'wealth' of 22:4. It may have been a Wisdom proverb where all four blessings come together: wealth, honor, life and blessing. These are the qualities that constitute the 'good life.' Since wealth is not the primary goal in life, these qualities can be enjoyed only when they are subordinate to Wisdom. Only by possessing righteousness does one acquire material prosperity and not the other way around. McKane translates צדקה as 'righteousness,' 'ethical fitness' and 'equity.'[10]

Most commentators translate the first צדקה as 'righteousness' and the second as 'prosperity.' Following the LXX McKane deletes the second צדקה.

11:19 - כן צדקה לחיים,   The establishment of good deeds brings life,

ומרדף רעה למותו.   but to pursue evil leads to death.

12:28 - באׄרח צדקה חיים,   In the path of good deeds life,

ודרך נתיבה אל-מות.   by way of its path there is no death.

16:31 - עטרת תפאׄרת שׄיבה   Gray hair is a crown of glory

בדרך צדקה תמצא.   it is attained by the way of good deeds.[11]

In all four passages צדקה is closely associated with longevity (life, old age).

According to Proverbs צדקה is what Wisdom possesses to bestow upon those who seek her. צדקה gives good life, long life, blessed with plenty and honor. It is the blessed life. This has been said to be the Hebrew equivalent of the Egyptian Maat.[12]

אׄרח צדקה of Proverbs is ארץ חיים, אׄרח/ארץ מׄישׄר of Psalms. That is where the goodness of God (טוב ה' – 27:13) awaits the righteous. In both literatures this 'land' comes from heaven (either from Wisdom or God Himself).

The difference is that in Psalms it is the sufferer who asks God to lead him to that path to be protected from real foes. In Proverbs, Wisdom promises anyone who wishes to seek her the blessed path that leads to contentment in living. The foes represent the ignorant. In Psalms צדקה is the end result.

Also, in Proverbs one needs to do what is right in order to achieve the good life (21:21).[13] In Psalms the emphasis seems to be more on being a devout person. We find another meaning to צדקה.

WONDROUS ACTS

צדקה appears in Psalms as the wondrous acts of God.

Ch. 71 - The poet opens with the hope that God's mighty acts (בצדקתך) will save and protect him (v. 2), so that he will continue to tell of them to everyone (vv. 15-19). He mentions צדקה five times: in the opening request—בצדקתך תצילני ('by Your attribute of saving acts You will save me'). In v. 15 צדקתך parallels תשועתך ('Your deliverance'); in vv. 16-17 צדקתך (here we should read צִדְקָתֶיךָ) parallels גברות ('mighty acts') and נפלאותיך ('Your wondrous deeds'); in v. 19 צדקתך follows גבורתך and is connected with גדלות; in v. 24 צדקתך stands as a concluding statement for his trust in God's acts, the same way as it appears in the introduction.[14]

The first צדקה refers to God's attribute of saving the devout persons as we have seen in Ps. 143. In v. 3 it is metaphorically compared to a rock and a fortress (מצודתי, סלעי, צור מעון). The other four mentions of צדקה refer to the power in action. It is His glorious deeds, how God came to the man's rescue, and how his enemies were punished. צדקה is associated with other words that indicate God's wondrous acts: תהלות, נפלאות, גדלות, תשועת, גבורת and זרע. These are צִדְקות 'ה, not on a national or universal scale, but on a personal level. The poet feels that by recounting God's saving acts he puts himself under their protection. צדקה is a *divine protective attribute through God's wondrous acts.*

In Ps. 111:2,3,6 and 7 צדקה is associated again with the acts of God (פעלו, מעשי ידיו, מעשה) and with 'His wondrous acts' (נפלאתיו) in v. 4. צדקתו עמדת לעד ('His attribute of saving acts is everlasting') refer to God, not man, as is the case in the next psalm. The conclusion of the psalm תהלתו עמדת לעד ('praise of Him is everlasting') in v. 10b provides an additional reason to understand צדקה as the wondrous acts of God. תהלות is what the psalmists recount as in 9:15, 71:14b-15,

78:3,4 79:13 and 106:2.

145:7 - זכר רב טובך יביעו   They shall recount Your abundant goodness

וצדקתך ירננו.   and shall sing joyously of Your saving acts.

In this psalm צדקה, in parallel with טוב, is associated with גדולה, מעשים, גבורות, נפלאות and נוראות (vv. 3-6), which are descriptions of God's acts in the universe. In v. 7 the poet sums up these acts that will be told and sung. In the second part of the psalm, the poet describes God's acts to man (vv. 14-20). It concludes, too, with the promise to recount them (תהלת ה'). צדקה in this psalm refers only to *God's Universal wondrous acts*, which are rooted in His goodness.

צדקה as God's saving act to man is also evident in Ps. 36.

36:7 - צדקתך כהררי-אל   Your saving acts are like high mountains

משפטיך תהום רבה,   Your laws like the great deep,

אדם ובהמה תושיע ה'.   man and beast You deliver, O Adonai.

God acts out of His righteous qualities of kindness, truthfulness, rightness and judgment. This kindness is a source of life (v. 10). The reading here should be in plural since the psalmist talks about saving acts, which well parallels 'Your laws'. These laws do not refer to a specific law in particular but to good laws in general. צדקה of v. 11, on the basis of the description in vv. 8-10, refers to the goodness of God which is the source of life.[15]

So is 22:32:

22:32 - יבאו ויגידו צדקתו   They will come to tell of His saving acts

לעם נולד כי עשה.   to people yet to be born, for He has acted.

The suffering poet promises to tell and praise God's past saving acts in public (vv.23,26) as a means to change evil people's behavior to fear and honor God. Only by learning of His power can people's whole attitude to fellowmen transform. Then they, in turn, will praise God and tell of His saving acts (vv. 28-32).

98:2 - הודיע ה' ישועתו   Adonai has proclaimed His victory

לעיני הגוים גלה צדקתו.   has displayed His saving acts in the sight of the nations.

This psalm calls the people to sing a new song to Adonai because 'He has done wonders' (v. 1). He saves His people not only because He is their God but because He is the ultimate judge. When it comes to universal justice He employs the same rule. צדקה, נפלאות and ישעה are used interchangeably.

103:6 - עשה צדקות ה'   Adonai executes saving acts

ומשפטים לכל-עשוקים.   and judgments for all who are oppressed.

צדקות and משפטים, דרכים ('ways') and עלילות ('deeds') are parallels. צדקה denotes the right, wondrous deeds God does which are mentioned in vv. 3-5,9-13.

40:11 - צדקתך לא-כסיתי בתוך לבי,   I have not kept Your saving acts to myself

אמונתך ותשועתך אמרתי,   I declared Your faithful deliverance,

לא כחדתי חסדך ואמתך לקהל רב.   I did not fail to speak of Your love and truth in a great congregation.

צדקה is connected with God's truth, deliverance, love, faithfulness and mercy (vv. 11-12).

51:16 - הצילני מדמים, אלהים, אלהי תשועתי,   Save me from bloodguilt, O God, the God of my salvation,

תרנן לשני צדקתך.   My tongue will sing forth Your saving acts.

The poet vows to tell the goodness of God, His past saving acts, thus attaining pardon and creating a new, clean heart for himself (vv. 9-14).

DIVINE GOODNESS

God's saving acts to his people and to individuals emanates from His goodness. We encounter this meaning in several passages.

Psalm 119 is a collection of individual sayings in an acrostic structure. Here צדקה appears twice (in vv. 40 and 142) in this meaning.

119:40 - הנה תאבתי לפקדיך,   See, I have longed for Your precepts,

בצדקתך חיני.   In Your goodness give me life.

In order to understand the message in this verse we may link it to other clauses such as 'ויבאני חסדך ה (v. 41a), meaning: 'With Your goodness give me life so that Your kindness will fall upon me. Or, we may connect it with בדרכך חיני ('in Your ways give me life'). Then צדקה parallels well with the idea discussed earlier of the blessed life. However, since the idea of good (משפטיך טובים) precedes בצדקתך חיני and חסד follows it, one tends to see here an associative thought of goodness that alludes to צדקה.

Verse 142 צדקתך צדק לעולם ותורתך אמת refers to the goodness of God as well.

89:17 - בשמך יגילון כל-היום   They rejoice in Your name all day long

ובצדקתך ירומו.   They are exalted in Your goodness.

Structurally, שם ('name') parallels צדקה but they are not synonymous. The people rejoice in His name or presence.[16] They exalt over His attribute of goodness and wondrous acts (גבורה and עז in vv. 14,18). These good acts are manifested through saving acts and fill the worshippers with confidence and happiness in knowing that when needed, He will come to their rescue.

72:1 - אלהים, משפטיך למלך תן   God, endow the king with Your laws

וצדקתך לבן-מלך.   the king's son with Your goodness.

King Solomon is asking God to give him the divine gifts of His attributes of justice (משפט) and goodness/righteousness, to enable him to use these tools to deal with his people in the right way (v. 2).

Verse 3 is problematic since its structure is uncertain:

ישאו הרים שלום לעם   May the mountains bring peace to (Your) people

וגבעות בצדקה.   and may the hills (bring them Your) divine attribute of

goodness.

שלום and צדקה are divine gifts. צדקה may be God's blessing of protection that brings about peace and abundance. שלום and צדקה parallel in an indirect way, if we understand the former as 'perfection.' Then it takes us back to the idea of תם, תמה ('perfect,' 'blameless,' 'righteous') that parallel צדיק and צדקה in Proverbs. However, it is sufficient to read the verse as a call to receive divine attributes in a sense of plenty, the way mountains and hills are portrayed as sources of abundance in Joel 4:18 and Amos 9:13.[17]

Dahood quotes a similar structure and idea from a Ugaritic text (51:v:100-1): "yblnn ǵrm mid ksp gbʿm lḥmd ḥrs" – 'the mountains did bring him much silver, the hills the choicest gold.'

Syntactically, the second colon in our verse does not parallel the first colon. Particle 'ב' is added to צדקה. Dahood offers another example where the verb is employed as the predicate of two successive clauses: in 66:20 הסיר ('removed') of the first colon governs the direct object תפילתי ('my prayer'). In our passage it is יששאו...שלום. In the second הסיר governs the accusative חסדו ('His love'), but is modified by the prepositional phrase מאתי. In our passage it is בצדקה.[18]

HUMAN GOOD DEEDS

PSALMS

As in the case of צדק, the divine צדקה is reflected in the human צדקה. This is evident in the following passages:

11:7 - כי צדיק ה', צדקות אהב,   For Adonai is righteous, He loves righteous deeds,

ישר יחזו פנימו.   the upright shall behold His face

צדקות refers to man's good deeds, as opposed to the evil deeds of the wicked described in vv. 2 and 5b.

The emphasis on the doing of these just deeds appears in 33:5 and 106:3:

33:5 - אהב צדקה ומשפט,   He loves justice and rightness

חסד ה' מלאה הארץ.   the earth is full of the kindness of Adonai.

Verse 4 states כי ישר דבר-ה' וכל מעשהו באמונה ('for the word of Adonai is right, His every deed is faithful'). דבר ישר refer to משפט while מעשי אמונה refer to צדקה. צדקה ומשפט emphasize the actual implementation of that attribute which constitutes goodness, the proper behavior in society. This צדקה ia a human attribute.

106:3 - אשרי שמרי משפט,   Happy are those who keep justice,

עשה צדקה בכל-עת.   who do right at all times.

The one who practices צדקה will witness the good fortune of Israel, His chosen people (v. 5a). צדקה is the good deeds, while משפט is not necessarily the law but a general term for justice.

The same meaning is found in Proverbs:

PROVERBS

We have already examined 11:19, 12:28 and 16:31. Here are additional passages:

10:2 - ,לא יעילו אוצרות רשע   Ill-gotten wealth is of no avail

וצדקה תציל ממות.   but righteous deeds save from death.

11:4 - ,לא יעיל הן ביום עברה   Wealth is of no avail on the day of wrath,

וצדקה תציל ממות.   but righteous deeds save from death.

Good deeds and morality are far more profitable than wealth acquired by wickedness. Wealth in itself is a blessing only when based on good deeds. Without righteous deeds wealth does not confer protection on the judgment day. Human rightness is the only effective safeguard of long life.

v. 5 - ,צדקת תמים תישר דרכו   The rightness of the blameless man smoothes his way,

וברשעתו יפל רשע.   but the wicked man is felled by his wickedness.

v. 6 - ,צדקת ישרים תצילם   The rightness of the upright saves them,

ובהות בּגדים ילכדו.   but the treacherous are trapped by their malice.

13:6 - ,צדקה תצר תם-דרך   Rightness protects him whose way is blameless,

ורשעה תסלף חטאת.   but wickedness subverts the sinner.

The idea in the above three passages is that performing righteous deeds guarantees the righteous person the 'straight' way (ארח/דרך ישר/מישר discussed above). It is a safe way. The evil person, on the other hand, will always fall as a result of his own evil deeds and desires. צדקה is powerful in that it can cause changes in the behavior and ways of man, and it can save the righteous.

11:18 - ,רשע עשה פעלת-שקר   The wicked man earns illusory wages

חורע צדקה שכר אמת.   but he who sows rightness has a true reward.

The efforts of an evil person, no matter how hard he tries, will result in emptiness. The righteous person, whose efforts are based upon his goodness, will reap true results.[19] צדקה is portrayed in agricultural terminology.

14:34 - צדקה תרומם גוי,   Rightness exalts a nation,

וחסד לאמים חטאת.   sin is a reproach to any people.

Righteous deeds exalt a nation, but sin is a disgrace[20] to a people. Or, doing sinful deeds leads to impoverishment of peoples and vice versa. This idea takes us back to Ps. 89:17, although there צדקה refers to God. In both passages there is a connection between צדקה and exaltation.

16:8 - טוב מעט בצדקה   Better a little with rightness

מרב תבואות בלא משפט.   than a large income with injustice.

Better to have little acquired through good deeds than to have plenty of revenue gained by injustice. The idea of wealth and rightness as a pair is repeated here. Again צדקה is associated with an agricultural activity.

v. 12 - תועבת מלכים עשות רשע,   Wicked deeds are an abomination to kings,

כי בצדקה יכון כסא.   for the throne is established by good deeds.

Wrong doing is hateful to kings, for only through righteous deeds will the throne be securely established. The connection between צדקה and the throne reminds us of Ps. 72:1. צדקה is constantly linked in Psalms and Proverbs with the verb עשה, which emphasizes action.

21:3 - עשה צדקה ומשפט   To do what is right and just

נבחר לה' מזבח.   is more desired by Adonai than sacrifice.

God prefers righteous deeds and the advocacy of justice to sacrifices.

Twice we find this meaning in Job.

JOB

37:23 - שדי לא-מצאנהו,   Shaddai, whom we cannot reach,

שגיא-כח ומשפט,   is great both in power and in justice,

ורב צדקה לא יענה.   the man abounding in good deeds He does not

torment.[21]

Robert Gordis' translation gives the verse the right structure and thought that we would expect from Elihu.[22] It is the clear-cut idea that whoever abounds in good deeds will not be affected by God. It may be right to emend רֹב to רַב to apply to a person and not to 'abundance,' as in 11:2 where הרב־דברים ('multitude of words') parallel איש שפתים ('a loquacious person').

35:8 - לאיש כמוך רשעך,   Your wickedness affects men like yourself,

ולבן-אדם צדקתך.   your rightness affects any man.

Wickedness is damaging mankind while good deeds benefit everyone. Driver and Gray suggest that only men, who benefit by the righteousness or suffer from the wickedness of their fellowmen, are rewarded by God.[23] This concept is rejected since the books of Job and Proverbs reiterate the basic idea that only those who practice goodness and righteousness are rewarded. One cannot be passive in life and yet be rewarded, even by mere suffering. Suffering is not a prerequisite for either being righteous or rewarded.

SOCIAL INTEGRITY

Very close to the meaning of צדקה as good deeds and goodness is its meaning of 'personal integrity' out of proper behavior and actions, as appears in the next two passages:

27:6 - בצדקתי החזקתי ולא ארפה,   I persist in my integrity and will not yield,

לא יחרף לבבי מימי.   my heart never harbored blasphemy.

By analyzing the text we may reach a slightly different interpretation: in 2:3,9 Job still holds fast to his righteousness ועדנו מחזיק בתמתו. תמה is explained as איש תם וישר ירא אלהים וסר מרע ('a blameless and upright man who fears God and shuns evil'). It is the opposite of חטא ('sin' – 1:22, 2:10). In 2:9 תמה is connected with blasphemy, as it is here with צדקה. In 27:5 לא אסיר תמתי ממני is synonymous with בצדקתי החזקתי ולא ארפה. In 31:6 תמה is Job's behavior as illustrated in detail throughout the chapter. צדקה, then, is the good behavior of a righteous person.[24]

צדקה may also mean 'innocence.' Job swears by God that he never uttered falsehood, nor declared his friends right. He holds fast to his innocence.

וישב לאנוש צדקתו. - 33:26   He restores to man his integrity.

Emending וַיָּשֶׁב ('he restores') to וַיְבַשֵּׂר ('he announces') or וַיְסַפֵּר ('he told') as suggested by some commentators, is uncalled for. The whole verse is simple: God is always willing to forgive the one who confesses his sin and sincerely repents. From the preceding verses, especially להגיד לאדם ישרו ('to declare a man's uprightness' – v. 23) and ישב לימי עלומיו ('let him return to his younger days' – v. 25) it appears that צדקה is a person's integrity, honorable position in society, his righteousness.

Gordis reads differently. He links v. 26c to v. 27a and reads: 'He recounts to men His goodness, and proclaims to men, saying...'[25] However, his explanation of why he reads וישב as 'recounts' is not clear. He does it probably in order to find a perfect parallelism between v. 26c and v. 27a.

MERIT

A familiar meaning, unexpected in poetry, appears in Psalms:

ותחשב לו לצדקה - 106:31   It was reckoned to his merit

לדר ודר עד-עולם.   for all generations, to eternity.

Only here do we find צדקה in Psalms as 'right,' as in Gen. 15:6. Verse 30 recounts Phinehas's act when in Ba'al Pe'or he interceded and the plague was stopped. This, v. 31 says, was counted to him as a merit for ever and ever. This merit granted the house of Phinehas the everlasting priesthood in Israel.[26]

Briggs explains צדקה quite properly as 'meritorious righteousness.'[27]

Summary: In Psalms, Proverbs and Job צדקה has several meanings, most of them relating to what is right and good.

In Psalms and Proverbs צדקה means 'the way of God,' which is straight and good. Those who are led onto this path acquire blessings of peace, protection, longevity, wealth and honor. These are divine gifts for the righteous and the wise who seek this path. It almost seems as though this is a real place (ארץ) somewhere on earth. It is the *divine protective sphere*. This place is reserved forever for them, and according to Psalms—also to those who suffer greatly and still retain their complete trust in God.

It is a state of being, a type of like where no wickedness can penetrate and affect the life of the righteous. It is the *blessed and protected life*.

As a result of this idea צדקה (also in its plural form of צדקות) has become the *saving acts of God*. These acts are wondrous and great. They are manifested not only in the life of mankind, but in the universe as well. Here it is associated with נפלאות ('wonders'), גבורות ('mighty victories'), גדלות ('great deeds'), תהלות ('glorious deeds'), תשועת ('saving acts'), מעשים ('great deeds') and נוראות ('awesome deeds').

צדקה has the connotation of goodness, since it is this divine attribute by which God manifests goodness. Goodness and rightness go hand in hand. It is the *goodness of God*. It is powerful in its capability and generosity. The righteous person asks God to be endowed with this attribute so that he can execute it on earth. When this is done, צדקה becomes the good deeds of man. The verb עשה is repeatedly connected with it. צדקה is the safeguard against evil. There is sense, merit and revenue in doing it. It safeguards the thrones of kings.

In Job צדקה is closely related to תמה, integrity, perfection, in terms of good thoughts and deeds in society.

Once it means 'merit,' which is more typical of the narrative literature. It may be that the author of Ps. 106 used this meaning because he was writing in a narrative form. Or perhaps his source was a prosaic text which he tried to transform into a psalm.

Although צדקה appears occasionally with משפט, it is not synonymous with it. משפט does not represent the law but is a general term for 'law.'

As in צדק, צדקה is related to 'straight.' Yet, in spite of its development in meaning, it has retained its meaning of what is right, straight and proper. It has nothing to do with the forensic field as צדק does. It emphasizes the ethical aspect of what is good and right in a more specific manner, with specific ideas. It underlines, as צדק, its divine source but emphasizes the *practice* of this attribute.

TABLE 5

Book	The Blessed Life	Right, good deeds of man	Divine goodness manifested through wondrous acts
Ps.	9	3	21
Prov.	1	14	–
Job	–	2	–

Book	Merit	Social integrity
Ps.	1*	–
Prov.	–	–
Job	–	2

*Ps. 106 has a narrative genre.

7

צדק
IN THE PROPHETS

1. SUMMATION OF PAST RESEARCH

Norman Snaith said that for the 8th century prophets צדק was the vindication of
the needy by God. It initially stood for the establishment of God's will on earth,
and secondly—for the establishment of justice on earth. It is partly משפט, the
known, strict ordinances and customs, and partly the ethical conduct emanating
from God, such as mercy and love.[1]

These prophets based their conception of righteousness (צדק or צדקה) on their
knowledge of God, and not on an ethical code. צדק, therefore, was a religious
term, like sin. Sin was rebellion against God, not against an ethical code.[2]

Olley, too, regarded צדק/ה as one and same term. In Deutero-Isaiah it is almost
synonymous with 'salvation' and 'prosperity.'[3] In the book of Isaiah he found that
it is more than just God's saving act. It involves His "action as being in terms of
the covenant relationship, resulting in harmony and right relationship." It
frequently occurs in contexts referring to a society where all, rulers in particular,
do acts of justice and righteousness according to the covenant stipulations.

Usually it is God who brings צדק/ה to man, through His saving acts (esp.
chapters 40-66). In some instances it is the ruler. In two cases the meaning is
forensic (5:23, 59:4 and perhaps 33:15), where it is the duty of the judge. צדק/ה
is a conditioned situation of balance.[4]

While examining the theory of the existence of the god Ṣedeq, Whitley concluded that for Deutero-Isaiah צדק became the "being of God": God's essence, power, plan, destiny, purpose and influence. It was Deutero-Isaiah who elevated the word to denote the essence of God.[5]

Ed Nielsen found that צדק and צדיק developed from the covenant theology. צדיק is the one who adheres to the conditions of the covenant. Like Olley he said that the setting of the רשע-צדיק confrontation was the kingship theology. This is evident in the stories of Saul, David and Absalom, and in Psalms (esp. 72).[6] Swetnam reached the same conclusion.[7]

As a result of military gains, the gap in the 8th century social classes widened, as Gordon wrote. Injustice took over in society. The prophets called for the restoration of justice. Amos saw צדק/ה as a living essence of social ethics in business and in court. Hosea saw צדק/ה as a prerequisite for חסד. Isaiah blended צדק with mercy. God acts in צדק and He expects the same from His people. Isaiah frequently equated צדק with salvation.

According to Malachi the light and warmth of this salvation act is described in שמש צדקה, meaning 'the saving grace.' For Deutero-Isaiah צדק/ה will come with salvation, as well as peace, prosperity, strength and joy. צדק/ה is also 'victory.'[8]

Rosenberg identified צדק in Deutero-Isaiah with the 'arm of God,' the salvation and vengeance of God.[9]

צדק to Amos, said Spiegel, was midway between philosophy and action, love and logic. It is not enough to define justice as the sum of virtues unless action has been added.[10]

Bollier said that for the 8th century prophets God's צדק/ה was manifested in two ways: physical deliverance from outside enemies and ethical deliverance of the righteous from the wicked from within. Amos emphasized particularly the legal aspect of justice in צדק/ה, while Hosea connected the ethical to the legal aspect. Isaiah stressed the forensic element in God's צדק/ה. If breaking the law of the covenant was פשע ('transgression') then adherence to the law was צדק/ה.[11]

Achtemeier said that the primary idea of צדק/ה of Deutero-Isaiah was that until God rejected Israel (by nullifying the covenant), Israel stood under the saving arm of God. Israel, contrary to her enemies, was always in the right, since her rights were deprived (54:14).[12]

Schrey tried to find a development in the 'righteousness of God.' The first stage of this philosophy took place when Israel saw צדקת ה' as divine saving acts, by delivering her from outside enemies. These military, victorious acts were recounted by the tribal league at watering places. The prophets aimed their demand for צדק at man, while holding the belief that God had still the power of securing צדק/ה on earth. Later, the idea of God's holiness and His saving righteousness was highlighted as the attitudes to which man should turn for help.

In Deutero-Isaiah God's righteousness is manifested in the restoration of Israel and Zion. This is demonstrated through the victorious acts of Cyrus, which are the victorious acts of God.[13] So again, צדק/ה is back to its first stage. The linguistic development has come full circle.

God's righteousness is revealed in the election of His people, as the prophets believed. Amos underlined this idea by saying that God could choose other groups, but because of His righteousness and several covenants (with the patriarchs and at Sinai) He chose Israel. God's צדק/ה is His active contribution to the existence and well-being of His people.[14]

2. EXAMINATION OF TEXT
ISAIAH

1:21 - צדק ילין בה   Justice dwelt in her
ועתה מרצחים.   but now murderers.

1:26 - אחרי כן יקרא לך עיר הצדק   Then you will be called "The City of Justice,"
קריה נאמנה.   "A Faithful City."

צדק is strongly related to justice as מלאתי משפט ('filled with justice') and the description of the perversion of justice in vv. 22-23 prove. Also, v. 26 talks about the restoration of righteous judges and counselors. Where justice used to dwell there are now murderers (a further indication of real crimes).

The equation of צדק with משפט and אמונה are very common parallels.[15] When all criminals and crimes are wiped out of Jerusalem, then the city will be restored to its faithfulness and truthfulness in justice of yesteryears. When law filled Jerusalem, justice dwelt in her. "Justice" is the general, just behavior relating mainly to courts but also to activities of business and of everyday life (vv. 22-23). Giving a new name represents a new chapter in life.[16]

Almost all commentators translate צדק as 'righteousness,' and משפט as 'justice.'

והיה צדק אזור מתניו - 11:5   Justice shall be the girdle of his loins,

והאמונה אזור חלציו.   and faithfulness the girdle of his waist.

Isaiah describes the coming of the child/king of David's house, who will launch a new era for Israel, for the world and for nature. It is a vision of an era of peace, justice and the universal knowledge of God. The vision opens with the description of 'the spirit of Adonai' that will rest upon this king. With this spirit he will judge his people. This justice is detailed in vv. 3-4: it concerns justice in court (judging the poor and the meek of the land, punishing the wicked) and preaching what is right to his people.

צדק and אמונה occur in parallel here as in 1:26 (אמן and צדק appear together also in 1:21). צדק, in Isaiah's eyes, intertwines with truthfulness. To what? To the spirit of God, to His essence and character. The king will 'delight in the fear of God' (v. 3a), that is, he will use the knowledge imbued in him as a guideline to deal with his people. This is what Solomon asked in Gibeon: "an insight to hear justice" (1 Kgs. 3:9,11).

Wearing צדק on his waist is similar to what we have seen above (p. 39).[17] Girding up clothes is done before undertaking any active work, like the soldier before going off to battle. Here the imagery suggests that the king will always be ready to execute justice.

צדק is a general term for just behavior relating to courts and to life in general. Targum and Rashi take this description symbolically: this king will surround himself with faithful servants. Kimhi explains that צדק and אמונה will be the king's strength.[18]

The waist, which symbolizes man's bravery, and the loins—man's fertility, are two basic elements of man's power and importance in society. To these two the prophet adds two values, as essential as the two symbols of manhood. Another possibility is that these two values can be seen as replacement for the symbols of manhood.

16:5 - ...וישב עליו באמת   And on it shall sit in truth...

שפט ודרש משפט   one who judges and seeks judgment

ומהר צדק.   and is swift in justice.

Chapter 16 is a prophecy about Moab. מהר צדק can be understood in two ways: מהר from מהר, ('fast', 'swift')[19] or from מהיר, ('expert,' 'competent').[20] Targum translates ועבד קשוט ('he executes truth') and the Jewish Publication Society (JPS)—'zealous for equity.'[21] The swiftness of the act shows expertise and competence. מהר צדק refer, then, to the king who will judge competently and justly. However, it may be understood as 'he will pronounce the verdict promptly and competently.'

It is the only time when מהר appears in a construct state and without yohd. It may have originally been either ומהיר לעשות צדק or מממהר לעשות צדק.[22] Haplography of 'מ' could occur, so 'י' is not necessary. Also, שפט and ודרש are in the present tense. שפט ודרש point to the process of conducting the case. מהר צדק show the manner of their completion. Therefore, צדק will be here simply another term for 'justice.'

26:9 - כי כאשר משפטיך לארץ   For when Your judgments are on earth

צדק למדו ישבי תבל.   the inhabitants of the world learn rightness.

משפטיך points to laws. צדק (in singular) is a general term for what is right. It is acquired through learning the divine laws.

v. 10 - יֻחַן רשע בל־למד צדק.   Let the wicked be forgiven, the one who does not learn rightness.

Shmuel Luzzatto explains vv. 9-10 interestingly: when God's laws are revealed in the land, the inhabitants learn what justice is. But when God does not keep His own law of punishing the wicked, then justice is absent in the land. The wicked will never learn to change their ways.[23]

It is difficult to see how Isaiah could ask God to show favor to the wicked. So commentators try to come up with other interpretations. Gray suggests reading somewhat like: 'no, the wicked will not receive favor,' by adding the negative word בַּל before יֻחַן.[24] He also suggests emending יֻחַן to read יֶחְדַּל ('will cease') following the LXX. The text, then, will be translated: 'The unrighteous shall cease to be, that learnt not righteousness.'[25]

Kimhi explains that the wicked do not learn justice because they do not believe in the existence of a divine purpose behind the events of life.[26]

Verse 10 elaborates on the character of the wicked and does not accuse God for letting them go unpunished. If indeed we have the text intact, then Isaiah hopes that when the inhabitants of the world learn God's laws, and thus His justice, then the wicked too will accept justice and consequently will be forgiven.

A more likely interpretation may be submitted if we read the text as a wish: 'The wicked, may they (never) learn rightness; they who sin in a land of integrity, may they (never) see God's majesty.' Perhaps at some point of copying the manuscript the letters בל were overlooked or deleted accidentally as a result of the preceding (ת)בל. This interpretation makes sense and fits well with vv. 9b and 11: the prophet hopes for the propagation of God's precepts among the nations (v. 9b) and at the same time he calls for a retribution upon the wicked nations (v. 11).

The word בַּל appears in couplets in vv. 14a and 18b. In vv. 10-11 it appears three times which may suggest an omission of one.[27]

צדק is what is done in נכחת ארץ. נכח means 'straight,' 'true,' a synonym for

ישר ('straight', 'upright'), which frequently parallels צדק. It is a general term for

what is right, as in the preceding verse. Again, צדק appears with the verb למד, to

learn.

11:4 - ושפט בצדק דלים   He shall judge the poor justly

והוכיח במישור לענוי-ארץ.   and decide honestly for the lowly of the land.

בצדק is the adverb of שפט. Its basic meaning is 'in the right, straight manner,'

to which the parallel במישור attests. We saw this in Lev. 19:15, Ps. 9:9, 96:13 and

Prov. 8:8.

צדק is the criterion by which a judge judges in the right way. In this unit צדק

appears twice: in our verse it directly relates to juristic range, while in v. 5 it

refers to what is right in general.

32:1 - הן לצדק ימלך-מלך   Behold, a king reigns for justice

ולשרים למשפט ישרו.   and ministers govern for judgment.

The preposition 'ל' in לצדק is interpreted in different ways. Most commenta-

tors read 'in'. According to Rashi it is the 'ל' of purpose:[28] 'in order to do justice';

It may indicate the outcome of an action: 'as a result of his rule the king

establishes justice.'[29] Another reading is the emphatic 'ל': 'surely a king rules

justly.'[30]

Isaiah, who emphasizes that the ultimate function of a king and his ministers

is to implement the law and thus do justice (1:26, 9:6, 11:3-5), says in our

passage: "Behold, a king reigns (to do) justice." Only the justice he performs gives

him legitimacy and the right to exercise his rulership. Because only then his people

can find refuge from injustice (vv. 2-8). צדק, then, is a general term for 'justice.'

The function of the ministers is to conduct the legal system (משפט) in a proper

manner.

HOSEA

10:12 - 'ועת לדרוש את ה   And it is time to seek Adonai

עד-יבא ויורה צדק לכם.   until He comes and rains a blessing.

Or, until He comes and teaches you rightness.

This is a difficult verse. Otto Procksch suggests inserting 'ה after ויורה for metric reasons. He also suggests to read יָרֶה for ויורה.[31]

There are several ways to read and explain this verse. The agricultural imagery is applied to the relationship between Israel and God. Just as one plows and sows in order to reap the harvest, so does one seek God to be answered favorably. How does one do this? By cultivating moral conduct.[32] The agricultural activities are symbols for action and result, for dedication and gratification. From Joel 2:23 and Isa. 45:8 it appears that there had been a connection between rain and צדק, probably rain with the right amount at the right time.

Hosea uses the same imagery in 6:3. In both cases the knowledge of God will come as rain (יורה, יבא גשם). However, in both passages יורה is not a noun but a verb. That is why Francis Andersen translates: 'He will water' (6:3) and '(He) rains' (10:12b).[33]

Bollier goes further: the land is the farm of God on which He sets Israel to produce for Him a harvest of righteousness and devotion. In this way God's own righteousness might find its fulfillment in blessing the earth.[34] This blessing is צדק. Pursuing this thought, James Mays translates it as 'salvation.'[35]

The idea of a divine rain which brings a blessing to the earth is probably a Canaanite metaphor, stemming from cultic mythology. In a message to Anat, Baal says: "Pour peace into the bowels of the earth, rain down love into the bowels of the fields."[36] From this and from language considerations T. Worden finds here a background of Canaanite fertility myths.[37] Martin Buss finds 10:12 to belong to cultic wisdom, where promises of blessings are typical.[38]

The LXX reads דַעַת ('knowledge') for וְעֵת ('and time'). Accepting this,

Hans Wolff translates: 'Break up the fallow ground of knowledge, and seek Yahweh, until the fruit of righteousness comes to you.' דעת, he says, fits well with the parallels of דעת, חסד and צדקה. For יוֹרֶה he reads פְּרִי ('fruit') as probably the LXX does (its reading may be תבואה–harvest), because the verb ירה in hif'il (to cause rain) is not attested in the Bible.[39] So also William Harper translates: 'fruit of righteousness.'[40]

The Syriac, Vulgate, Artur Weiser and Emanuel Halpern[41] translate: 'he will teach justice/righteousness.' Harper also recognizes this as a possible translation.

צדק, suggests James Ward, may mean 'one's right' in the sense of 'salvation.' But more probably it means 'justice,' which fits with 'teach.'[42] Rashi and Kimhi offer both possibilities and explain the metaphors.[43]

Hosea plays on the words ירה and צדק and gives them double meanings: 1. He alludes to rain since he uses agricultural imagery. יורה צדק, then, will denote 'the right (amount) of rain.'[44] 2. 'He will teach you rightness.' This relates to seeking God on one hand, and to רשע ('evil'), עול ('iniquity') and כחש ('deceit') on the other, as a contrast.[45] ירה in hif'il (to teach) is very common (48 times). Isaiah, Hosea's contemporary, says יורה דעה in 28:9 ('he would give instruction'), and in 9:14—מורה שקר ('who gives false instruction'). See also Hab. 2:18.

צדק here is a blessing given to man by God. But it is conditional. Man has to prepare his moral ground wholeheartedly in order to be blessed. The connection between water/rain and divine blessing is strong, probably stemming from cultic ceremonies, adopted by the prophetic and Wisdom theologies. This theology was no doubt carried on through Deutero-Isaiah (45:8). In 2:21-24 Hosea reiterates this idea: after renewing the covenant and knowing God, He will send blessings from the sky (the rain) to bless the earth. Here too he uses agricultural imagery: God will sow Jezreel in the fertile land.

2:21 - וארשתיך לי בצדק ובמשפט,   And I will espouse you to me with righteousness and judgment,

ובחסד וברחמים.   with love and with mercy.

Instead of the bride-price Israel will receive God's attributes: צדק, משפט, חסד and רחמים. In return, Israel will be forever faithful/truthful to Him, and will accept the divine instruction. To know Him constitutes an intimate relationship, starting at the marriage taking place at the signing of the covenant.

אמונה ודעת, חסד ורחמים, צדק ומשפט are three couplets. All these attributes had been the basis for the original covenant that was rejected by Israel. Hosea uses the former couplet as we have seen before in the Psalms.[46] Can we deduce from this that the phrase צדק ומשפט, which reflects the totality of justice (written law and behavior/morality), is a Hoseanic concept, adopted by the prophets of Judah? Was it he who gave צדק the meaning of 'blessing,' which was later employed by the South? It is quite conceivable.

צדק for Hosea is divine ethics, manifested in blessing man, probably as part of the covenant stipulations. This צדק is confined solely to God, unlike Isaiah's צדק. Their approach to צדק is from two different points of view.

בצדק is not an adverb as in other cases, but serves as a noun.[47]

ZEPHANIAH

2:3 - בקש צדק, בקש ענוה,   Seek rightness, seek humility

אולי תסתרו ביום אף-ה'.   that you may hide at the day of Adonai's wrath.

2:1-3 is the continuation of chapter one. In vv. 2-3 Zephaniah offers a chance of deliverance before 'the day of the wrath of God' will fall upon Judah. He addresses 'the meek of the land,' who followed the divine ordinance. He advises them to seek Him by seeking צדק and ענוה. Probably ענוים were originally the poor. Later the word received the meaning of righteous people. In many psalms the poor and the righteous are identical. Now, in Zephaniah's time, they are called צדיקים or חסידים.

Zephaniah, in Josiah's time, reflects the later interpretation. These ענוים have been doing God's law, but he cannot guarantee them a salvation, because the destruction will be so devastating.

John Smith maintains that Zephaniah talks to all the Israelites of the world. בקש את ה' and בקש צדק are identical: securing God's favor is done by seeking righteousness and humility. He also asserts that vv. 2b-3 are a gloss from the exilic or post-exilic period.[48]

Verses 2-3 are integral parts of the prophecy. The prophet encourages the righteous, in the face of disaster, not to lose faith, to seek the ethical teaching and humility. For Zephaniah 'rightness' and 'humility' are the two most important values to possess. Hosea concentrates on צדקה, חסד, דעת and צדק.

בקש את ה' parallel בקש צדק בקש ענוה. This shows that these two values emanate from God himself. It is the only place where humility is a divine attribute. It is not impossible to arrive at this idea, since man's values reflect those of the deity. צדק appears as a general term for morality. God is willing to extend His attribute of righteousness to save those who have been righteous all along.

JEREMIAH

11:20 - וה' צבאות שפט צדק   But Adonai of Hosts, a just judge,

בחן כליות ולב.   assays feelings and thoughts.

31:22 - יברכך ה' נוה צדק,   May Adonai, the Just Abode,

הר הקדש.   The Holy Mount, bless you.

50:7 - תחת אשר חטאו לה',   For they have sinned to Adonai,

נוה-צדק ומקוה אבותיהם.   The Just Abode and the Hope of Their Fathers.

In these three texts צדק appears in a construct chain. It is also an element in the name of God. The epithet שפט צדק is found also in Ps. 9:5, where צדק was translated as an adjective. צדק has no change in vowels whether it functions as a noun or as an adjective.

John Bright's translation of 'who judgest aright,'[49] that of Samuel Driver 'that judges righteously,'[50] or that of Sheldon Blank 'righteous judge'[51] are closer to the Hebrew than 'a judge of justice/righteousness.'

Jeremiah prays that God may punish his adversaries, who are in effect God's enemies. He argues his case before Him, the universal judge, because no feelings or thoughts escape Him. God is called upon to come to the defense of His own value of justice. In a real court situation, Jeremiah feels, he will have no chance for justice. The confidence of Jeremiah in the righteous judge echoes Abraham's plea in Gen. 18:25: השפט כל-הארץ לא יעשה משפט ('Shall not the Judge of all the earth do justice?').

The translation of 'just' is preferable to 'righteous' in order to underline the sense of justice in a court setting. Also, the word ריב ('dispute') points to a legal field.

In 31:22 Jeremiah envisions the time when Israel returns to Judah, then each one will bless the other with a new blessing. God is mentioned by two of His attributes: justice and holiness. He is identified with the Temple Mount and probably with the city of Jerusalem (see Isa. 1:26, Zech. 8:3). This identification, strengthened by the prophecy of future bliss, gives the listener a sense of eternity and security.

נוה צדק may be another epithet for the Temple Mount or for Jerusalem. However, this epithet will be God's own in the return of Zion. The leadership of Judah, at the moment, is unjust and untrustworthy. The future trust will be well justified, since the trust will be not in man but in God alone. He is the source of justice, holiness, security and peace.

There must have been a connection between the idea of holiness and justice as found in Priestly literature and in Isaiah and Jeremiah. The prophets probably adopted this Priestly theology.

The translation of נוה צדק among commentators is divided between 'righteous adobe' (Bright) and 'habitation of righteousness/justice' (Driver, Binns, Cunliffe-Jones, Gordis and Freedman). Elmer Leslie gives צדק the sense of abundance and translates: 'prosperous habitation.' This is a name for the whole land of Judah.[53]

Ernst Nicholson translates without explanation: 'Your true goal,' as God's name.[54] Kimhi explains the new blessing as referring to Judah, who is righteous and holy.[55]

The divine abode is where rightness dwells. In the words of the psalmists this place is the divine throne (89:15, 97:2), the right arm of God (48:11) or heaven (85:12).

Jeremiah believes that in the age of the future bliss God will bless His people through His attributes of justice and holiness. נוה צדק is a descriptive means to express this idea: an attribute and its dwelling in the divine sphere. The translation of 'just' indicates its association with justice.

The same epithet and meaning are found in 50:7. Instead of holiness, Jeremiah uses the term מקוה. Twice he calls God מקוה ישראל (14:8, 17:13), an expression unique to our prophet.[55] He uses מִקְוֵה and not תִּקְוָה to express the same idea he presented in נוה צדק: a place and an attribute which are united in God.[56]

22:13 - הוי בנה ביתו בלא-צדק Woe to him who builds his house with no justice

ועליותיו בלא משפט. and his upper rooms with no legality.

Jeremiah accuses Jehoiakim of social injustice and of lavish building while the country is in political and social turmoil.[57] He accuses the king for not following his father's conduct: Josiah judged his people according to the law. He knew God (vv. 15b-16). Jehoiakim thinks only about personal gain. He sheds the blood of innocents (v. 17), and does not pay the laborers who have built his home (v. 13b). He ignores the law.

Bright translates בלא צדק 'unfairness,' בלא משפט 'wrong.'[58] 'Unfairness,' which denotes the ethical aspect of injustice, is preferable to 'unrighteousness' (Driver, Bennett, Binns and Freedman).

As in Psalms and Proverbs, צדק ומשפט stand for the two aspects of justice, thus the term becomes a hendiadys.

23:6 - וזה שמו אשר יקראו And this is the name by which (God)

ה' צדקנו. will call him: Adonai is our justice/salvation.

33:16 - זֶה אֲשֶׁר יִקְרָא-לָהּ   And this is what she will be called:

ה' צִדְקֵנוּ.   Adonai is our justice/salvation.

Both passages are imbedded in prophecies that promise the establishment of a righteous king of the House of David, in the time of the future bliss. In both passages the time of this king's reign will be marked as the age of salvation and security.

The problem is: what is the king's name? Is it ה' צִדְקֵנוּ or צִדְקֵנוּ? It is unusual to have 'adonai' as an element in a man's name. Elements like יְהוֹ, יָה or יָהוּ (יְהוֹצָדָק, צִדְקִיָּה, צִדְקִיָּהוּ) were common. Also, יִקְרָאוֹ needs a subject, probably 'Adonai.' If so, then a word is missing between Adonai and צִדְקֵנוּ, perhaps מלך ('king'). However, since both passages lack this term, ה' צִדְקֵנוּ is probably original.[59]

The name צִדְקֵנוּ is unusual too. This form is not otherwise attested in the Bible. ה' צִדְקֵנוּ have the same meaning as צִדְקִיָּהוּ or יְהוֹצָדָק. Bright suggests that this construction is "an old formula which preserves the original verbal force of Yahweh...which was not understood in the 6th century BC."[60] The LXX probably reads צֶדֶק which does not solve the problem. The Old Greek text reads יוֹצֶדֶק/ יְהוֹצֶדֶק[61] probably in order to smooth the text.

Names similar to ה' צִדְקֵנוּ (names of the deity and/or names with pronominal suffixes) are the following: אֵל גִּבּוֹר (9:5), ה' נִסִּי (Exod. 17:15), ה' שָׁלוֹם (Jud. 6:24), ה' יִרְאֶה (Gen. 22:14). As we can see there is no name structure of Adonai + verb/noun + pronominal suffix plural for a person. The closest to this form is ה' נִסִּי. For Jeremiah, in the days of salvation, there will be a change of names: of land, vow, king and God.[62] ה' צִדְקֵנוּ is the actualization of the repeated formula of the Deuteronomist: אֲשֶׁר נִקְרָא שְׁמִי עָלָיו ('which bears My name').[63]

Although ה' צִדְקֵנוּ will be the king's and Judah's name, it is used to emphasize that 'God is our (ultimate) justice.'[64] Jeremiah bonds the Davidic righteous king with the future righteous city. A similar idea is expressed by Isaiah in 1:26 where he links the righteous leaders to the righteous Jerusalem.

From the above discussion צדקה would be then a general term for the divine

righteousness.

EZEKIEL

3:20 - ...ובשוב צדיק מצדק ועשה עול   And when a righteous man turns from his

rightness and does injustice...

צדק stands in contrast to עול ('injustice'). When Ezekiel wants to use the root

צדק to reflect actions of rightness, he uses צדקה and its plural form, as in v. 20b.

He also states that the one who once behaved in the right way, but has now turned

to evil, will stumble for his way will no longer be straight. This idea reminds us

of צדקה in Wisdom literature, e.g., Prov. 11:5,6 and Ps. 5:9. Ezekiel may have

given צדק this idea, while confining acts of justice to צדקה. But still צדק has

retained its general meaning of right behavior which is symbolized by a straight

path.

Ezekiel's צדק is merely an earthly, secular behavior.

45:10 - מאזני צדק ואיפת-צדק   Right balance and right ephah

ובת צדק יהי לכם.   and right bath you shall have.

Our attention is immediately drawn to the legal texts in Lev. 19:36 and Deut.

25:15. The measure bath takes the place of hin. Just stones are omitted. Ezekiel

addresses this prophecy to the princes of Israel who carry out injustice. He asks

them to use just weights and measures as written in the law. As a priest he knew

the law and its terminology. His צדק is basically what is right, proper and just.

The prophet elaborates on the rightness of weights and donations in vv. 11-15. The

contrast to צדק is the general term for injustice—עול, as appears in the legal

literature of Leviticus (19:35), Deuteronomy (25:16) and Ezekiel (3:20).

Ezekiel has retained the original meaning of צדק while extending it to its

secondary meaning of what is right morally, in the legal and general behavior

spheres.

DEUTERO-ISAIAH

צדק appears 17 times in Deutero-Isaiah. These will be divided between Israel's
and the divine צדק.

HUMAN צדק

51:1 - שמעו אלי רדפי צדק,   Listen to me you who pursue rightness,

מבקשי ה'.   who seek Adonai.

v. 7 - שמעו אלי ידעי צדק,   Listen to me you who know rightness,

עם תורתי בלבם.   a people with My teaching in their heart.

Those רדפי צדק are synonymous with מבקשי ה'.[65] The verbs רדף and בקש
denote the process of searching while acting, like the commandment צדק צדק תרדף
('justice, and only justice, you shall pursue'). The law does not suggest only
pursuit but action. Those ידעי צדק (those who know the real meaning of justice) are
one step ahead of רדפי צדק (those who are in the process of pursuing the meaning
of justice). They have reached the goal of pursuit. It is part of their existence.

Both verses point to one thing: צדק is to be found in the divine sphere. If they
pursue and carry out the divine will, they will surely find צדק. In both cases we
have action and result, as in Hosea and Zephaniah.

צדק is תורה. This teaching, as we learn from the prophets, consists of the
divine will which is doing justice, loving God, protecting the downtrodden and so
on. In short, doing what is right in God's eyes in order to keep this people in
harmony with each other and with Him. So is the neutral phrase בקש ה'.
Consequently, צדק is what is right according to God's teaching. This state of
rightness shields them from human contempt and insults (v. 7), since they have
acquired part of the divine moral power. Also, the nature of צדק is eternal while
insults are temporary.

As mentioned before, most commentators see no difference between צדק and
צדקה. They differ on the question as to whether they are ethical or eschatological.

That is the reason for variations in their translations. For example, for רדפי צדק some translate 'you who pursue deliverance' (John McKenzie, Elmer Leslie, George Knight), while others translate 'righteousness' (Thomas Cheyne, John Smith, G. Wade, Solomon Freehof, Edward Young, Reuben Levy, John Skinner, C. von Orelli). For ידעי צדק McKenzie translates 'you who know righteousness,' Leslie—'what is right' and Knight—'you who have experienced (my) saving activity.'

Christopher North's translation comes closest to the text: 'endeavor after right, who seek the Lord.' This confirms the ethical emphasis of צדק. He feels that in the end the ethical and eschatological threads are quite entangled, since those who do right are saved. For ידעי צדק he translates 'you who know and do what is right.' 'You who know' is insufficient because the knowledge of God involves also experience and action.[66]

Olley sees here a salvific emphasis because Abraham, with whom God made a covenant, is mentioned as a model. According to him צדק is the saving purpose of God.[67]

Since תורה encompasses the ethical as well as the legal teaching of God,[68] צדק is what is ethically right. It is the apex of the divine teaching. There is no eschatological nuance at all.

59:4 - אין קרא בצדק   No one pronounces (the verdict?) by way of justice,

ואין נשפט באמונה.   no one is judged by way of truthfulness.

In this prophecy Deutero-Isaiah accuses Israel of ethical and legal sins, from murder to false witness. The 'calling' has to be associated with the judicial process since he charges that no one is judging truthfully. The calling comes to invoke justice for action. Since אמונה is a noun, so is צדק. The verb נשפט ('is judged') points to the corrupt judges as do the rest of the accusations. We would expect אין שפט באמונה ('no one judges truthfully') to match with the first colon.[69] No one calls for justice in court, or no one pronounces a just verdict.

61:3 - ,וקרא להם אילי הצדק   And they will be called "The Oaks of Rightness",

מטע ה' להתפאר.   the planting of Adonai to glorify Himself.

As in Isaiah and Jeremiah the new era of peace for Israel will carry also new names: "The Oaks of Rightness," "God's Priests," "The Servants of God" (v. 6). There is no legal connotation but a general term for rightness. The planting of Israel in her renewed land gives צדק a sense of eternity as in 51:7. The same idea is found again in 60:21. Oak trees stand for strength and durability.

The preposition 'ל' following a verb indicates in Hebrew an indirect object, while the preposition 'ב' following a verb indicates an adverb as in 59:4.

62:1 - עד יצא כנגה צדקה   Until her vindication emerges like a bright light

וישעתה כלפיד יבער.   and her salvation will burn like a torch.

62:2 - וראו גוים צדקך   Nations shall se your vindication

וכל מלכים כבודך.   and all kings your glory.

From the parallelism it seems that צדק means ישועה and כבוד. But this is not so. This צדק will come out as a bright light which refers to vindication in a court setting. In Ps. 37:6 we find a similar expression והוציא כאור צדקך.[70] When God goes out to exonerate Israel, the first step will be a change in Israel's legal status: from sinner to innocent. Then salvation and glory will follow and will be revealed to all nations.[71] An additional outcome of this vindication will be a new name (vv. 2b,4b).

64:4 - פגעת את שש ועשה צדק   You have hurt (?) him who rejoices and does

rightness

בדרכיך יזכרוך.   they who are mindful of Your ways.

This is a difficult verse and passage. The chapter talks about God's anger with everyone, including those who do right. One reading is that God met the one who does right, who is also happy and mindful of His ways. This does not make sense since the prophet laments the sins of all, even those of the righteous. The word פגעת may not mean 'met' but 'hurt'. The righteous are waiting (v. 3) for the change in the present conditions of suffering and depression. From this we can deduce that עושה צדק is the one who does right in the general sense, who walks in God's ways. צדק points to the divine sphere ('Your ways').

Most commentators translate צדק in our verse as 'righteousness' and explain that God meets (favorably) with those who do righteousness.[72]

Freehof, following Rashi, Kimhi and Ibn Ezra, explains that the righteous is the one who in past cases interceded for the sake of Israel.[73] James Smart asserts that God brings rejoicing to those who do right.[74] But this is not so. It is through rejoicing that the righteous do right.

58:2 - ,ישאלוני משפטי-צדק   They ask Me for the right laws

קרבת אלהים יחפצון.   they are eager for the nearness of God.

The search for God is to know His will, His ways and His right judgments and laws. In short, the desire is to be close to God. משפטי-צדק have the same syntax as שפטי-צדק (Prov. 16:13). Deutero-Isaiah accuses Israel of hypocrisy: they do search for right judgments but not in order to act upon them but to cover up and hide behind their social iniquities (vv. 4,9).

v. 8 - ,והלך לפניך צדקך   Your rightness will walk before you,

כבוד ה' יאספך.   the glory of Adonai behind you.

On the basis of 52:10 and our verse an emendation in the reading of the verb יאסף is called for. The appropriate reading is יַאַסְּפֶךָ, in pi'el, which means 'He will walk behind you,' rather that in pa'al, which means 'He will gather you.' The reading in pi'el parallels well with its preceding colon which talks about 'walking in front.'[75]

צדק is compared to the bright light of dawn (cf. 62:1). Following 52:12, should we read צִדְקוֹ, instead of צִדְקֶךָ, thus referring to God? Probably not. The preceding passage describes the desired ethical behavior of Israel (vv. 6-7) vis-à-vis their present hypocritical behavior (vv. 2-5). This צדק is the ethical conduct of man. 'Rightness' encompasses what is right and honest in every situation. Self-respect and pure intention are here emphasized.

DIVINE צדק

41:2 - ‏מי העיר ממזרח צדק,‏ Who has roused justice from the east,

‏יקראהו[79] לרגלו?‏ summoned him to His feet?

Instead of צדק some commentators read צדיק (after LXX and Vulgate) and translate: 'Who has raised up a righteous one from the east?'(e.g. McKenzie, Bollier). Cyrus is the object of the prophecy although he is not mentioned. Whitley emends the text as follows: ‏מי העיר(ו) ממזרח בצדק יקראהו לרגלו‏, explaining that "God calls cyrus in accordance with His divine plan." The addition of the particle 'ב' is in accordance with 42:6, 45:13.[76]

Smart rejects the translation of 'victory' and the theories that the deliverer is Cyrus or Abraham. He suggests, on the basis of v. 9, that the subject is Israel in the messianic time.[77] Other exegetes see God or צדק as the subject of the verse.

The subject is no other than God, since the answer to 'who' is given in v. 4: ‏אני ה'‏. God, in a court setting, comes to prove His intervention in world events.

There are several ways to interpret our verse. Here are two suggestions:

1. God raised up צדק from the east and called it to His feet. We may have here a survival of the pagan belief concerning the sun-god šmš, which rises in the east.[79] The sun-god was considered the god of justice. God overcame[79] צדק and brought it to His feet, a symbol of victory.[80] The connection of the verb עור and צדק appears again in 51:9. Deutero-Isaiah brings forward this mythological event because this prophecy is to be delivered to the nations of the world. The prophet deals in the same way with other mythological creatures. When he addresses Israel these mythological allusions are not used.

2. ‏(ב)צדק ממזרח מי העיר צדק יקראהו‏ - The object is Cyrus. God calls him rightly or through His attribute of righteousness (as in 42:6, 45:13). By this attribute God causes political changes. The word לרגלו may be a duplicate from ברגליו in v. 3.

Based on 1 Kgs. 25:42, Hab. 3:5 and Gen. 30:30, Luzzatto interprets in the following way: in justice God calls Cyrus to follow Him, להגלו being 'after him.'[82]

Again, קרא is associated with צדק.

42:6 - אני ה' קראתיך בצדק, I, Adonai, have summoned you in My righteousness,

ואחזק בידך. and I have held you by the hand.

Again the verb קרא comes with צדק and צדק is connected with the right hand, this time Israel's hand (see also v. 13). This call is in the name of the divine righteousness, as in the second suggestion above.

41:10 - אמצתיך אף-עזרתיך, I strengthen you and I help you,

אף תמכתיך בימין צדקי. I uphold you with my right hand of righteousness.

צדק, as God's protective power, is underlined.

45:13 - אנכי העירתהו בצדק I have roused him in righteousness

וכל דרכיו אישר. and I have leveled all roads for him.

God calls Cyrus to action with His righteousness. By doing so He empowers him with identity and validity. Deutero-Isaiah links God's צדק with straight ways (see 64:4 above) in the same way as Wisdom uses the human צדקה.

42:21 - ה' חפץ למען צדק, Adonai desires for the sake of His righteousness,

יגדיל תורה ויאדיר. that He may magnify and glorify His teaching.

In vv. 17-20,24 Deutero-Isaiah accuses Israel for being a people who rejected the teaching of God. Nonetheless, he wants to save His people who are at present oppressed (v. 22), not because they have repented but in order to keep His teaching alive. It is His attribute of righteousness that must be kept intact and powerful.

The idea seems to be that if God neglects to take care of His people, His righteousness is marred and loses its value and strength and perhaps even its validity. The prophet also seems to imply that all this cannot take place as long as Israel remains in a contemptible situation.

Some exegetes doubt the genuineness of v. 21 because it disjoins the continuation between vv. 18-22 and vv. 22-25. But this is not so. The prophet wants to emphasize that God, in spite of Israel's sins, will act in her favor, although for His own reasons. What He will do to change the situation is described in 43:1-12. Smart explains that v. 21 summarizes vv. 1-9 where "God has been pleased to magnify His Torah." למען צדק could be translated "because of the justice that is intrinsic to His nature."[82]

צדק, says Young, "bestows mercy according to God's purpose...(it is) manifested in the putting away of sin." In so saying, Young also sees צדק as a divine, powerful attribute which is activated by God's wish and goodness.[83]

Kimhi explains that למען צדק comes to demonstrate that the glorification of the Torah will be done not for the sake of Israel but for the sake of God. Targum sees צדק as the vindication of Israel.

45:19 - אני ה' דבר צדק,   I am Adonai who speaks the truth,

מגיד מישרים.   who utters what is right.

Both צדק and מישרים refer to 'true words' in contrast with the lying and cheating described in the preceding cola. Against what is hidden and wrong, God declares what is true and above-board.[84] צדק stands for light while lying stands for darkness. 'The situation in life' of דבר צדק is that of a court setting.[85] God is the teacher of the law (cf. 26:9). In all cases where דבר appears with a direct object, there is no particle 'ב' that follows it.[86]

Conversely, Smart explains צדק as 'salvation,' "the righteous order that will prevail on earth when God's will is sovereign." This צדק is in an eschatological context where the juristic meaning has been lost.[87]

Skinner sees in צדק the ethical quality of trustworthiness and sincerity by which God has revealed Himself to His people.[88] He and Wade[89] view צדק as the correlation between words and deeds. God is true to His promises. צדק is what is true and honest.

As for the term מישרים, צדק and אמונה which parallel each other, H. L. Ginsberg suggests the interpretation of 'kindness,' 'graciousness.' He bases this reading on Ps. 88:12-13, 96:10c,13bc and 98:9. In all these passages the verb that appears with them is either שפט or דין ('to judge'), which he explains as 'provide for' and not 'judge.'[90] The same interpretation applies to צדקה and משפט ('care,' 'providence') in Ps. 36:7-8.

45:8 - הרעיפו שמים ממעל,   Drip down, heavens, from above,

ושחקים יזלו צדק.   and let clouds pour down blessings.

צדק is compared with rain of goodness that fertilizes the land. According to the Deuteronomistic theory God's blessing of rain and the fructification of the earth correlate with the righteous behavior of Israel. However, as in 41:10 and 42:6 there is no prerequisite on the part of Israel to change its evil ways. This goodness depends on God's will alone, to prove His uniqueness to all. צדק is the means to this proof.

God is "carried away" by His own description of His powers of creation. He commands the heavens to activate צדק over the earth, so that the earth in turn will bring forth its blessings. There is a chain of cause and effect. This salvation that emerges from the earth has nothing to do with the eschatological idea of salvation.

Knight retains his interpretation of צדק as 'saving activity' "which is to burst up from below as well as...from above."[91] How can saving activity burst from below? The prophet's salvation or any other divine activity stems directly from God Himself.

Levy translates צדק as 'right' (noun), which is "the heavenly embodiment of truth, justice and morality.[92] In other words, this is the overall righteousness of God as interpreted in this research.

Whitley deviates from 'divine rule' and translates here 'divine decision.'[93]

51:5 - קרוב צדקי,   My vindication is near,

יצא ישעי,   My salvation has come out,

וזרעי עמים ישפטו.   and My arms will judge nations.

McKenzie translates צדק as 'victory' and ישע as 'deliverance.' In 45:8 he translates צדק as 'righteousness' and ישע as 'victory.' This demonstrates his struggle with these two words. He also prefers the LXX translation, even though the Hebrew is clear.[94] זרוע ('arm') and ימין ('right hand') in 4:10 are associated with צדק and משפט, which explains צדק as the attribute of power that is manifested in justice.

Ginsberg reads צדק here, as in 96:13 and 98:2-3, as 'providence,' משפט as 'provide for,' while זרועי (either plural or singular) as God's means by which He extends His 'help' or 'benefaction' (ישע or ישועה).[95]

DANIEL

The word צדק appears only once in Daniel, in the prophet's prayer.

9:24 - .ולכפר עון ולהביא צדק עלמים   And to expiate iniquity and to bring an ever-lasting rightness.

צדק עלמים is a unique phrase. This phrase is part of the 'seventy weeks' prophecy. Nothing in the verse helps to shed light on the exact meaning of צדק. The words עון, חטאה and פשע ('iniquity') are mentioned together in Exod. 34:7, where Moses describes God as forgiver of sins. כפר ('expiate') and משח ('anoint') are words referring to priestly religious functions (Lev. 16:17,27,32, Exod. 29:29, Num. 3:3). Six actions will be taken by God pertaining to Israel, the prophets and the priests. God will straighten out the Israelite society and with it He will bring an eternal rightness (coming right after listing various types of sins). 'Rightness' represents moral and legal conduct. צדק denotes a general term for both aspects of justice.

Since Daniel was greatly influenced by past prophets, צדק עלמים is understood as the way they perceived the new era: when the right relationship between man and God is firmly and truthfully established. This new covenant will be forever—ברית עלם.[96] צדק עלמים may be Daniel's understanding of ברית עלם.

D.S. Russell explains צדק as righteousness that covers three aspects: legal justice, salvation-victory and moral holiness of God that is manifested in His righteous dealings.[97] This צדק, according to E.W. Heaton, entails two meanings:

the salvation of Israel from external foes and the restoration of moral righteousness in Israel.[98] Driver equates צדק עולמים with Deutero-Isaiah's תשועת עולמים ('everlasting salvation'–45:17). The idea may be the same: the abolition and forgiveness of sin and the perpetual state of righteousness.[99]

James Montgomery's translation of 'rightness' and that of Raymond Hammer's 'right' describe the essence of צדק in our verse well.

Summary: For Isaiah צדק is basically connected to a law and court setting. It appears with משפט or the verb שפט. However, as its closeness with אמונה demonstrates, he expands its meaning to encompass all ethical behavior in society. It is connected with faithfulness to the spirit of God, to His will and essence. To do injustice is to reject Him.

The righteous person is portrayed as wearing צדק. In this respect צדק is a *state of being*. It is a means by which one judges rightly (בצדק). It is strongly associated with the character of the king. It gives his reign legitimacy, respect and stability.

For Isaiah צדק is an earthly condition with a vague allusion to a divine value. It is quite difficult to discern between the human and the divine צדק. The laws (משפטים) are divine, while צדק is the result of learning them.

Ezekiel's use of צדק is similar to that of Isaiah. For him, too, צדק is an earthly moral behavior, symbolized by a straight path. Also, as a priest he uses צדק as a legal term for what is right in terms of balances and weights.

Between Isaiah (8th century BCE) and Ezekiel (6th century BCE) צדק has gone through some changes. Hosea, Zephaniah and Jeremiah retained the judicial aspect of the word, but at the same time they have elevated it to the divine sphere. This is carried to such an extent that Jeremiah calls God 'the abode where the attribute of justice dwells' or 'the just abode.' Zephaniah parallels God with צדק and ענוה: to seek God is to seek His attribute of rightness and humility, as well as to carry out His laws.

For these prophets צדק comes directly from God. It is His attribute that embodies all the blessings people need for a happy and prosperous life. When צדק comes down there is a perfect balance between man and earth, man and man. But it does not come automatically. One has to seek it through learning and doing good acts. The idea of blessing is similar to that of צדקה in the Wisdom literature, though less developed.

צדק is a divine attribute among others such as: משפט ('judgment'), חסד ('love,' 'kindness'), רחמים ('mercy') and אמנה ('faithfulness,' 'truth'). When Israel will be ready for a renewed covenant it will be signed through these attributes, צדק being the most important, for it embodies every conduct that is right and just. Jeremiah develops this divine concept much further: צדק is the essence of God, His being, His goodness. He coins new terms to underline the utmost supremacy of God:-מח־ צדק and מקוה ישראל to denote that God is the ultimate place, source and attribute of rightness.

As Isaiah before him, Jeremiah connects צדק with the king's functions. However, the righteous king will only come in the messianic age.

Deutero-Isaiah links the human צדק with the divine attribute but gives the latter much more emphasis. It is the power to vindicate Israel and protect her. Through this act He glorifies His name. Daniel's צדק is close to that of Deutero-Isaiah. It is God's overall power of rightness that includes forgiveness and blessings.

Many of the prophets employ צדק in its original meaning. They all use it as a general term for what is right, just and proper. When on earth, it is what man has to be and do (עשה). When on high, it is the attribute through which the goodness of God is reflected and ready to be actuated. The world will be a more pleasant place to live. צדק is kept in heaven for the righteous only, but Deutero-Isaiah deletes this condition.

צדק and divine holiness are closely related. It is a Priestly theology adopted by the prophets.

Deutero-Isaiah uses 'light' as a metaphor for צדק.

TABLE 6

Book	Rightness of God	Rightness of man	Rightness of king	Blessing
Isa.	2	6	4	–
Hos.	2	–	–	1
Zeph.	1	–	–	–
Jer.	5	1	2	–
Ezek.	–	1	–	–
Deut.-Isa.	10	3	–	1
Dan.	1	–	–	–

Book	Truth	Rightly, justly	Right, just	Vindication
Isa.	–	1	–	–
Jer.	–	–	3	–
Ezek.	–	–	3	–
Deut.-Isa.	1	2	1	3

8

צדקה
IN THE PROPHETS

The word צדקה appears 77 times in the prophetic literature, almost half the times in which it appears in the Bible.

ISAIAH

10:22 - בּליון חרוץ שוטף צדקה.   A destruction has been decreed washing away
blessings.

The destruction of Israel will be almost total and only a remnant will survive. Its force will be like a consuming flood.

The word צדקה is quite problematic. It does not parallel a word or an idea to give us a clue to its meaning. Hence the various translations, such as: 'retribution' (JPS),[1] 'righteousness' (Freehof, Leslie, Skinner et al), 'justice' (Orelli, Herbert et al).

The LXX has a different version: כּי (הוֹא) מכלה דבר וחרוץ בצדקה—'(God's) destructive force is done in righteousness.' This is rejected by Mosheh Goshen-Gotstein.[2] Other translations, such as Targum, Peshita and the Arabic version, and some commentators add the preposition 'ב' like the LXX. This changes the noun to an adverb but still does not clear the difficulty in understanding the text.

Some commentators connect vv. 21-23 to 2:6-22 and 5:15-16 which are original to Isaiah. In these prophecies Isaiah says that by the destruction of Israel (people and land) the way to the recognition of God's moral kingdom will be paved. So here too, they explain, שוטף צדקה refer to Israel's destruction, not

Assyria's. For Bollier the phrase refers to two sections in the Israelite society: בליון ('destruction') refers to the sinners and צדקה ('righteousness') refers to the righteous.[3]

שוטף צדקה is understood in two ways:

1. The destruction will be so complete that no righteousness will be left on earth. It will be executed in the name of the divine righteousness. As Kimhi explains: it is right that the destruction should be decreed because the people of Israel are sinners. However, he believes, it refers specifically to the ten lost tribes. שאר ('remnant)') are the people of Judah in the time of Hezekiah who returned to God and were saved from Assyria. He sees the prophecy as a past event.

2. Rashi sees it differently: although the destruction was decreed, nevertheless the righteousness of the repenting remnant will wash it away and delay its coming.[4]

I present another possibility for consideration: the decree will ignore the pleading of the few righteous so that it be rescinded. Their acts of righteousness will not change the decision. It does not mean though that blessings or acts of righteousness will cease forever.

The following suggestion is the most plausible: the phrase בליון חרוץ שוטף צדקה does not belong to the unit of vv. 20-22a. Logically it will fit after v. 11, and the prophecy of almost complete destruction of Assyria in vv. 16-19 fit the concluding statement of a total destruction. However, שוטף צדקה can only refer to Judah since Judah, and not Assyria, was the recipient of the divine צדקה. The total destruction will wash the *benefits* and *blessings* God bestowed upon her.

If we pursue this thought, and Bollier's, a new suggestion emerges: בליון חרוץ will come after כל הארץ ('all the land/people'), to refer to the Assyrians in a separate prophecy, while שוטף צדקה will come after אל גבור ('mighty God') of the preceding verse. שוטף צדקה describe the act of the glorious God who will overflow His true remnant with blessings. צדקה is the opposite of בליון. The verb שטף usually refers to water (e.g. Isa. 28:2, 66:12, Ezek. 13:11), which is considered as a source of blessings to nature as well as to man.

Isaiah uses the imagery of water as a destructive force quite often.[5]

28:17 - ושמתי משפט לקו   And I will put the law as a measuring line

וצדקה למשקלת.   and truth as a plummet.

Verse 17a stands in contrast to v. 15c: משפט and צדקה are the replacement of כזב ('falsehood') and שקר ('treachery') of v. 15. Isaiah uses צדקה in a judicial setting. It may be that he uses it in the same way as צדק, namely, 'truth' as against 'falsehood.' Or, since he uses קו (masculine) and משקלת (feminine) as parallels, משפט (masculine) corresponds with קו and צדקה (feminine)—with משקלת. Consequently, צדקה is thrust into a juristic field of צדק and the use of צדקה is employed for stylistic reasons only.

Isaiah parallels צדקה and משפט six times, צדק and משפט—three times. As opposed to the behavior of lying, God will install a new state of behavior: this time a behavior of truthfulness. The foundation of the new society will be based on law and truth (in court, most probably). משפט וצדקה will be the criteria for the new society. The two terms refer to legal morality.

33:15 - הלך צדקות   He who performs righteous deeds[6]

ודבר מישרים.   and speaks the truth.

This verse is very similar to 45:19. The verb נגד ('to speak,' 'to announce') replaces the verb הלך ('to walk'), which makes a better parallelism. In 11:4 צדק ('justice,' 'truth') parallels מישר ('honesty'). Here is the only time where the verb הלך parallels the verb דבר. הלך appears with the nouns דרך and ארח ('path,' 'way') in 2:3 and 30:21. The omission of דרך or ארח in our verse (הלך בדרך צדקות) may have occurred for stylistic considerations.

Speaking the truth is compared to walking in the straight, right way. Two concepts are combined into one. The psalmist parallels דבר with פעל/עשה—to do—in 101:7, 15:2 and 109:20 which is the basic idea in our passage. The rest of the verse explains what הלך צדקות is: it means refraining from acting unjustly against the law. In order to emphasize the idea of actions Isaiah uses the plural צדקות and parallels it with the plural מישרים (there is no occurrence of the singular דבר מישר). מישרים here means 'truth' as אמת ודבר צדק ופעל in Ps. 15:2.

Another possibility is that Isaiah uses צדקה in place of צדק in order to parallel with the plural מישרים and מעשקת ('fraudulent dealings') for poetic reasons. צדקה has a legal meaning.

Luzzatto, too, explains הלך in the sense of doing,[7] and so does Kimhi. He also suggests that the particle 'ב' is missing. Rashi explains הלך as 'he who loves.'

Isaiah restates his thought from 32:17-18 that acts of justice will result in security (see vv. 16ff).

exegetes translate צדקה and מישרים as adverbs: righteously/justly and uprightly/honestly respectively. Only Arthur Herbert conceives צדקה as 'righteousness' and translates: 'the man who lives an upright life and speaks the truth.'[8]

32:16 - משפט במדבר ושכן   Justice shall dwell in the wilderness

צדקה בכרמל תשב.   and rightness shall abide in the orchard.

והיה מעשה הצדקה שלום   The act of rightness shall be peace

ועבדת הצדקה השקט ובטח.   and the work of rightness—quietness and

security.

Here is the classic Jewish conviction that through righteous acts (מעשה and עבדה) peace and security will dwell on earth. The law (משפט) will be the guideline for actions. צדקה is the cause for a peaceful living which is righteous acts.[9]

33:5 - נשגב ה' כי שכן מרום,   Adonai is exalted for He dwells on high,

מלא ציון משפט וצדקה.   He will fill Zion with judgment and rightness.

The effect of משפט וצדקה will be truthfulness, strength, salvation, wisdom and the knowledge of God. The unit is a prayer imbedded in Wisdom thinking. When Isaiah describes Judah's past as מלאתי משפט צדק ילין בה ('she was filled with equity, justice dwelt in her'—1:21), he emphasizes the current situation where judges and officials are engaged in criminal acts. Now the prophet is calling God to fill Zion again with the same משפט וצדקה.

צדק and צדקה seem to be indiscriminately used in our unit for 'justice.' However, here it is associated with blessings and knowledge, so more likely צדקה stands for the knowledge of what is right ('יראת ה—'the fear of Adonai'—concludes what will be the desirable behavior and acts of Israel). This is the first time we encounter the idea that God causes rightness to fill Zion. However, it is not clear whether Isaiah ascribes 'rightness' to a divine source or to man. It seems that the former, in this case, is more plausible.

Isaiah uses the same style in 32:16-17 where he mentions משפט וצדקה but elaborates only on צדקה. Here, too, he describes משפט וצדקה as filling Zion ('dwelling in her') and again he uses the verb שכן. He sums up צדקה as 'יראת ה. For Isaiah משפט וצדקה is a hendiadys, in the like of שיש ושמחה ('rejoicing and merriment'—22:13) and השקט ובטחה ('peace and security'—30:15).

9:6 - להכין אתה ולסעדה   To establish her and support her

במשפט ובצדקה.   with judgment and (acts of) rightness.

Again there is the connection of rightness with peace. The king, with the knowledge of what is right, will establish his kingdom. צדקה means acts of rightness.

Deutero-Isaiah as well uses a variety of verbs that mean 'support' (עזר, אמץ, תמך, החזיק ד׳ – see 41:10, 42:6) with the divine צדק as an attribute of power. Isaiah uses the verb סעד ('support') in conjunction with צדקה, a human attribute of doing justice.

1:27 - ציון במשפט תפדה   Zion will be redeemed with equity

ושביה בצדקה.   and her dwellers—with (acts of) rightness.

In vv. 25-26a God describes how He will cleanse Israel from her sins. In v. 27 the prophet uses a passive tense. The question is: whose משפט and צדקה—God's or Israel's? Since God is the active party in the unit and since he is the one who restores justice to Zion, it is reasonable to assume that משפט וצדקה are His tools

of action. They are His "cleansing material." However, whenever God acts, the
verbs are in active voice: אָשִׁיבָה ('I will cause to return'), אֶצְרֹף ('I will
cleanse'), אָסִירָה ('I shall remove'). Then comes a passive verb יִקָּרֵא: another
party will call Zion "The City of Justice." Consequently, it is more likely that
תִּפָּדֶה ('she will be saved') refers to Israel whose right acts (which God brought
about) will redeem her. Also, the subject of the following verbs (יְכֻלּוּ, יֵבֹשׁוּ, תַחְפְּרוּ,
בַּחַרְתֶּם) is also Israel. The source of מִשְׁפָט וּצְדָקָה is God's and the acts are Israel's.

Verse 27 opens a new unit which ends in v. 31. While the preceding unit
accuses Israel of legal injustice, here the accusation concerns idolatry. It may be
that פּשְׁעִים וְחֹטָאִים ('transgressors and sinners') in v. 28 contrast with מִשְׁפָּט while
עֹזְבֵי ה' ('those who forsake Adonai') contrast with צְדָקָה.[10] This means that those
who walk in the way of God are those who possess or perform צדקה (similar to
הלך צדקת). So again צדקה is associated with the knowledge of what is right, the
knowledge of God, which leads to performing right deeds. צדק of vv. 21 and 26
refers specifically to legal justice, while צדקה refers to acts of justice.

Targum understands צדקה as those who do (follow) the Torah (i.e. 'יראי ה).
Kimhi too explains צדקה as actions.[11]

The translation of Isaiah's thought will be as follows: 'the righteous in Zion
will be redeemed by performing right deeds according to the teaching of God.'
There is no allusion whatsoever to messianic age, as Orelli suggests.[12]

5:7 - ויק למשפט והנה משפח,   He hoped for judgment, but behold, violence,

לצדקה והנה צעקה.   for justice, but behold, a cry.

The word צעקה usually refers to the outcry of the oppressed.[13] This puts צדקה
in a judicial context. The word צדק would be more appropriate as in 1:21, 16:5,
26:9,10. We may assume that Isaiah uses צדקה for assonance effect to match צעקה.

5:16 - ויגבה ה' צבאות במשפט   Adonai of Hosts is exalted in Judgment

והאל הקדוש נקדש בצדקה.   and the Holy God is sanctified in rightness.

Isaiah introduced the prophetic idea of the holiness of God, originated in his vision and call (6:3).[14] The holiness of God emphasizes the immorality of man. According to Snaith this holiness is the "inner Nature of Deity" which demands morality of people. The phrase האל הקדוש נקדש בצדקה explains the connection between God's holiness and His righteousness. People realize this idea by the exaltation of righteousness in their midst.[15]

The loftiness of God (in character and location)[16] stands distinctly in contrast to the lowliness of the sinners (v. 15).[17] The high (גבהים) among Israel can be made low but God's loftiness is always secure. It is the ephemeral against the eternal, the instability against security. How Does God maintain this position of holiness and loftiness? By His attributes of משפט וצדקה.

Verses 11-12 describe the inebriate behavior of a certain segment in the society, who pay no heed to God's existence. Their indulgence in wrong and destructive conduct contrasts with משפט וצדקה. There is no reference to legal wrong.

The essence of Isaiah's message is that only through moral acts can one approach the holiness of God. Holiness is inherent in morality.

The thought in our passage suggests that to be exalted is not only a divine reality but it can be materialized by man too.

Until then, the belief was such that by being holy the deity separates himself from man. He is approachable only through rituals. Now Isaiah adds a new thought: God is approachable through His essence, which is His צדקה, an attribute that stands for a code of behavior. It elevates man to the divine sphere.

A further thought is deduced here: Isaiah views the punishment of the haughty as the act of this moral code.[18]

Luzzatto explains that נקדש בצדקה means that His holiness will be revealed through the same punishment which, for the oppressed, is צדקה.[19] Rashi, too, separates משפט and צדקה: משפט refers to the punishment of the wicked; צדקה refers to God's sanctification among the remaining righteous.[20]

צדקה is the moral code of behavior and acts.

מצדיקי רשע עקב שחד - 5:23   For a bribe they acquit the guilty

וצדקת צדיקים יסירו ממנו.   and revoke the innocence of those in the right.

The prophecy attacks the drunken judges, who pervert judgment because they are unable to see right from wrong. They also take bribes to pronounce the guilty innocent and the innocent guilty. They deny justice to those in the right. Their behavior is against all that God teaches (v. 24c). צדקה refers to judicial setting with a specific meaning of *innocence*. It is used the same way as in Ezekiel, but carries a different meaning (e.g. 18:20, 33:12).

The word צדק should have been used in place of צדקה, but this could disturb the rhyme and assonance of the verse. It is awkward to say וצדק צדיקים. Isaiah could say מרשיעי צדיק but he never uses this phrase. He plays on the root צדק: מצדיקי ,צדקת, צדיקים. In order to use צדק in a construct form Isaiah uses צדקת. It appears that he does not distinguish between צדק and צדקה when it serves his stylistic needs as a poet.

AMOS

ההפכים ללענה משפט - 5:7   You who have turned judgment to wormwood

וצדקה לארץ הניחו.   and cast (deeds of) rightness to the ground.

If we link this verse with vv. 10-15, the word משפט would refer to a court setting (שנאו בשער מוכיח–'they hate the arbiter in the gate',דבר תמים יתעבו—'they detest him whose plea is just', אביונים בשער הטו—'they subvert in the gate the cause of the needy', והציגו בשער משפט—'display justice in the gate') while צדקה refers to righteous deeds in society, especially in regard to the unprotected (בושסכם על דל —'you imposed a tax on the poor', משאת בר תקחו ממנו—'you exact of him a levy of grain', צררי צדיק לקחי כפר—'you enemies of the righteous, you takers of bribes', שנאו רע ואהבו טוב—'hate evil and love good'). For Amos משפט וצדקה is an idiom that encompasses all aspects of social justice, which is the teaching of God. Good behavior will render them life (דרש טוב...למען תחיון; דרשו את ה' וחיו; דרשוני וחיו).

—'seek Me and you will live'—vv. 4,5,13).

Henry McKeating describes צדקה well: it is more than rectitude and justice. It includes also benevolence and kindness, especially to the poor and the innocent.[21] The missing word in his explanation is 'deeds.'

6:12 - כי הפכתם לראש משפט   For you have turned judgment to poison

ופרי צדקה ללענה.   and the fruit of (deeds of) rightness to wormwood.

This verse is very similar to 5:7 in words and meaning. The parallelism here is better. The differences are mainly two: the address is direct, in second person plural; the wicked not only engage in perversion of justice but prevent good deeds, whenever they are performed, from taking effect. They turn the sweetness of צדקה to bitterness. In thus doing, they prevent blessing from falling on the righteous and the needy. The blessing is life itself.[22]

Mays equates פרי צדקה with משפט saying that צדקה is the source of משפט. משפט is done when the right relationship among people is the normal quality of life.[23]

According to Amos, says Wolff, צדקה designates behavior of a righteous man, who defends another who is in the right, who has been wrongly accused. The wicked turn this order of justice into a repulsive state.[24]

5:24 - ויגל כמים משפט   Let justice well up like water

וצדקה כנחל איתן.   and (deeds of) rightness like an unfailing stream.

Amos rejects festivals, sacrifices, cultic songs and music. He prefers 'equity and righteous deeds.' Water brings blessing of fertility, food and life in general. Water is smooth, abundant, constant, with no impediments, as justice in society ought to be.

MICAH

6:5 - .'למען דעת צדקות ה   In order to know God's saving deeds.

Micah describes events in the history of Israel in which God saved His people. The phrase צדקות ה' refers to these glorious saving acts in history.

7:9 - ‏עד אשר יריב ריבי ועשה משפט,‎   Until He takes up my case and executes my judgment,

‏יוציאני לאור אראה בצדקתו.‎   He will vindicate me, I shall see His vindication.

Judah confessed her sins, but she leaves her case to be judged by God Himself. She is certain that God will prove her innocent through His attribute of צדקה—His code of rightness. צדקה is justice in action. The divine righteousness is analogous to His vindication of Judah. Another interpretation is that Judah will again witness the divine blessing.

But there is a more likely explanation to our verse. We have here four stages of a case presented in court:

1. The case (ריב) is presented.
2. The case is being judged (‏ועשה משפט‎).
3. The verdict is announced: innocent (‏יוציאני לאור‎).
4. The innocence of the accused (צדקה) is revealed to all (‏ותרא איבתי‎—'and my enemy saw'—v. 10).

Since the legal terms ‏ריבי‎ ('my case'), ‏משפט‎ ('my judgment'), and ‏יוציאני‎ ('He will vindicate me') refer to the prophet/Judah, צדקה ought to be in the same grammatical form, namely ‏צדקתי‎ ('my innocence').[25] The innocence of Judah is the main concern of Micah. It is necessary that Judah's reputation, self-esteem and belief be restored, to discomfit the mocking enemies. By proclaiming Judah innocent, God's power will be revealed as well.

This explanation is very similar to that of Ps. 17, where the conclusion is that it is the poet's hope to spiritually behold (‏חזה‎) God after he is acquitted (see pp. 37-38).

Bollier and others see צדקה in both 6:5 and 7:9 as saving acts of God according to His covenant. Salvation is manifested by forgiveness.[26]

HOSEA

10:12 - ‏זרעו לכם לצדקה,‎   Sow for a blessing

קצרו לפי חסד.   reap for goodness.

The phrase יורה צדק in v. 10b posed a problem in interpretation, so much so that two separate translations were suggested (see pp. 84-85).

The word חסד parallels צדקה. These two attributes are derived by seeking God. They are the opposites of רשע ('evil'), עולה ('injustice') and כחש ('deceit'). רשע is connected with bad politics (כי-בטחת בדרכך ברב גבורך...ביום מלחמה)—'for you have relied on your way, on your host of warriors...on a day of battle'—vv. 13-14). In 6:6 Hosea parallels חסד with the knowledge of God (cf. 4:1). Analogously צדקה is associated with דעת אלהים too. The phrase דעת אלהים stands against idolatry, assimilation and sacrifices (4:10-14, 5:4,7, 6:6, 7:8, 8:13). In 3:5 (and also in 8:3, 14:3) the search for God is the search for His goodness. צדקה, then, has no connection with justice. The prophet uses משפט to denote a forensic context (5:1, 6:5, 10:4, 12:7). If צדק means blessing, then its feminine form means the same unless it was used in order to avoid repetition. If indeed they mean the same, then צדקה means goodness[27] and blessing.

Mays connects צדק/ה with the knowledge of God.[28]

McKeating does not see צדקה as the reason for sowing, but the tool with which to achieve חסד: 'Sow for yourselves in justice and you will reap what loyalty deserves.' He understands it as a proverbial saying.[29] This interpretation is far from the original.

Buss explains that this is a cultic Wisdom aphorism where "promises of blessing are typical." צדק, צדקה and משפט are "equivalent to divine order...which can be paralleled with שלום...or טוב."[30]

Targum translates the agricultural images as analogies of acts in life: 'Do for yourselves good deeds.'

JOEL

2:23 - כי נתן לכם את המורה לצדקה,   For He has given you the early rain for blessing,

ויורד לכם גשם מורה ומלקוש.   and brought down for you rain: the early and

the late rain.

Joel describes the fertility of the land which will yield abundant crops (vv.
19,22,24,26). He uses the imagery of rain to symbolize abundance of blessings to
Zion. מורה is probably another word for יורה of a local dialect. There is no allusion
to 'teaching'[31] as in Hosea 10:12, only to blessings by rain. It does not even have
to be an analogy, but actual rain that will fertile the land.

I suggest that Joel, as Hosea, plays on words. While Hosea plays on צדק and
צדקה, Joel plays on מורה. מורה is The Teacher, God Himself, who brings blessings
to man through rain—מורה. The word את may be omitted.

Wolff translates לצדקה not 'for' but 'according to (covenant) righteousness.'
He translates המורה as 'food' because LXX, the Old Latin version and Peshita
presuppose the word מאבל ('food'). He points to 1:16 where אֹכֶל parallels שׂמחה
וגיל and to the reference of 2:21-24 to chapter one, where the consumption of the
crops by locusts is described. To support his interpretation he quotes the Rabbinic
tradition that sees the first rain as a teacher (מורה) to instruct the people to prepare
for the winter season.[32]

Kimhi explains that the rain (יורה) is a token for forgiveness. Close to this
explanation is Julius Bewer's translation: 'He has given you food as (a token of
your) justification.' The renewal of this nourishment shows the reestablishment of
the right relationship between God and His people.[33] צדקה, then, is the exoneration
of Judah, signified by abundant food.

Driver translates לצדקה 'in just measure' (the rain). Ibn Ezra rejects the
meaning of המורה as 'teacher' and explains it as rain which gives comfort and
healing, after Mal. 3:20.

To summarize Joel 2:23, the commentators offer two different explanations to
צדקה: 1. The righteousness of God. 2. The justification, forgiveness of Judah. The
interpretation suggested here is to understand צדקה as the divine blessing of Judah

through ample, seasonal rain.

JEREMIAH

The word צדקה appears eight times in Jeremiah, six times the phrase משפט

וצדקה (five times with the verb עשה-'to do'). In all passages צדקה is a human

action relating to the law, but it is unmistakably a divine source. Jeremiah clearly

states that צדקה is part of God's act on earth, an action He would like Israel to

espouse.

9:23 - כי אני ה'   For I, Adonai,

עשה חסד משפט וצדקה בארץ,   do kindness, equity and (acts of) rightness in

the world,

כי באלה חפצתי.   for in these things I take delight.

These words express the prophet's conviction that God exercises His teaching

not only in heaven but on earth as well. Maimonides learned from vv. 22-23 that

the highest achievement of man toward perfection is by learning God's justice and

purpose.[34] In order to create a secure society, man has to take God as his model.

To know Him is to realize that God rules the universe, nature and mankind.[35]

22:3 - כה אמר ה':   Thus said Adonai:

עשו משפט וצדקה.   do equity and (acts of) rightness.

23:5 - ומלך מלך והשכיל   He shall reign as king and shall prosper

ועשה משפט וצדקה בארץ.   and he shall do equity and (acts of) rightness in

the land.

33:15 - בימים ההם ובעת ההיא   In those days and in that time

אצמיח לדוד צמח צדקה,   I will raise up a righteous branch of David's line

ועשה משפט וצדקה בארץ.   and he shall do equity and (acts of) rightness in

the land

What is the meaning of משפט וצדקה? Jeremiah explains this very clearly in

22:3. It is social justice: to save the oppressed, help the helpless, disengage from

violence and murder of the innocent. A member of the society must be active in maintaining a healthy, just society, where court is the place to exercise what is right. In v. 16 Jeremiah repeats this demand: Josiah, he argues, took charge of the poor. When they needed justice he himself saw that they were protected. This is the essence of knowing God, as expressed in v. 16: הלוא היא הדעת אתי הלוא—'that is truly knowing Me.' Because Josiah did משפט וצדקה, he enjoyed the good life: הלוא אכל ושתה...אז טוב לו '(your father) ate and drank...then he was well' (v. 15).

In 23:5 (33:15) Jeremiah says that as a result of the king's doing משפט וצדקה Judah will be saved and peace and security will reign over her. Here, as in 9:23, knowing God (השכל) is the first step that leads to doing משפט וצדקה.

For Jeremiah this idiom is clear. It is social justice that leads to a good life for the individual as well as for the nation. The laws are the teaching of God. משפט comes first since it denotes civil laws. צדקה joins in to create an idiom of wholeness: do *what is right*. Carrying out the law is underscored.

33:15 is parallel to 23:5. In 33:15 the king is צמח צדקה and in 23:5 he is called צמח צדיק. Some scholars emend this to צמח צדק/ה and translate: 'a legitimate offspring.' This interpretation is rejected since Jeremiah had no doubt about the legitimacy of that future king, for he will be chosen by God from the House of David (33:17).

The title of צדיק or צדקה underlines the ethical character of that king. This emphasis is also shown in his name: ה' צדקנו. God will bring forth (an agricultural term) a righteous king[36] and a righteous nation. Righteousness will eternally secure the dynasty and the priesthood (vv. 17-18,22). A 'righteous shoot' is the best translation of צמח צדקה. This צדקה refers to doing משפט וצדקה and to Jeremiah's vision of social justice.

4:2 - ונשבעת חי-ה'   And you shall swear "As Adonai Lives"

באמת במשפט ובצדקה,   in truth, justice and rightness,

והתברכו בו גיים ובו יתהללו.   nations shall bless themselves by Him and praise

themselves by Him.

Commentators differ in the translations of באמת במשפט ובצדקה as to whether they are nouns or adverbs. As for ובצדקה the translations are varied such as:'rightly' (Bright), 'in uprightness' (Emil Kraeling), 'in righteousness' (Freehof, Annsley Streane, Elliott Binns, Driver, Harry Freedman). משפט וצדקה should be understood as in the previous passages. Line three probably alludes to Ge. 12:3.

51:10 - הוציא ה' את צדקתינו; Adonai has revealed our vindication;

באו ונספרה בציון את-מעשה אלהינו. come let us recount in Zion the deed of Adonai, our God.

If indeed צדקתינו (plural) is correct then it means 'our good deeds,' as against Babylon's sins. If the Syriac and Targum are correct (they read צדקתנו in singular), then the meaning will be 'our vindication,' as in Micah 7:9 (read אראה בצדקתי). However, the two parts of the verse do not fit. The intention is to tell of God's deed(s)—מַעֲשֵׂה or מַעֲשֵׂי, and צִדְקָתִי would be more appropriate. Also, the unit describes the impending punishment of Babylon, which is the act of God. Punishing Israel's enemies and recounting them are God's צדקה.

Nevertheless, another possible interpretation may eliminate this incongruity. 'The act of God' is the bringing forth of Israel's vindication. Her vindication is in contrast with משפטה, Babylon's judgment (her guilt). For this interpretation צדקתינו should be emended to צִדְקָתֵנוּ. Innocence is revealed but acts are recounted.

As Amos (5:15,24), Micah (6:8), Zephaniah (2:3), Isaiah (33:5), Psalms (99:4) and Proverbs (21:3), Jeremiah uses משפט וצדקה as an idiom to denote the whole idea of social justice. For him the difference between צדק and צדקה is quite notable: both refer to social justice (see 22:13) but while צדק is specific to the law, צדקה is more inclusive: the ethical aspect of justice is underlined by being active in its implementation.

צדק can also be an adjective or an element in the epithet of god. צדקה is associated with the knowledge of God that leads to good life. It is connected with the words טוב, חסד and משפט (cf. Prov. 21:3,21). For Hosea and Zephaniah צדק is associated with the knowledge of God but Jeremiah allots this meaning to צדקה and wraps it with Wisdom philosophy.

As Wisdom teaches, he correlates it with the king. He also uses צדקה in its meaning of 'vindication,' again a clue to its link with the law. As Hosea (10:12), Joel (2:23), Amos (6:12), Proverbs (11:!8) and Deutero-Isaiah (61:11), Jeremiah uses צדקה in an agricultural metaphor.

EZEKIEL

The word צדקה appears in Ezekiel twenty times. The prophet uses משפט וצדקה eight times in a repetitive way.

18:5 - ואיש כי-יהיה צדיק   If a man is righteous

ועשה משפט וצדקה...   and he does equity and (acts of) rightness...

In vv. 5-8 the prophet explains the term משפט וצדקה. It comprises two aspects of covenant rules: not worshipping other gods and keeping the laws concerning such issues as adultery, robbery, usury, paying a debt, providing the needs of the poor and judging truthfully. In short, keeping 'statutes' and 'ordinances.' This is repeated several times. Whoever does משפט וצדקה is considered a צדיק, a person who does not engage in idolatry (vv. 6,15). Doing משפט וצדקה prolongs one's life (v. 9). For Ezekiel 'life' is not in terms of quality (the way Wisdom teaches) but the opposite of death (vv. 16-19).

45:9 - חמס ושד הסירו   Make an end to lawlessness and rapine

ומשפט וצדקה עשו.   and do equity and (acts of) rightness.

The idiom משפט וצדקה is the opposite of חמס ושד. This is followed by additional examples of what is משפט וצדקה: put a stop to your exactions of My people, keep right measures and weights. He warns the leaders against tyranny.

In all, משפט וצדקה are manners of behavior and deeds in society according to the covenantal ordinances and statutes given by God. Mostly, these are laws to be kept in order to assure life and social stability. They create an idiom that stands against sinful deeds whether secular or religious. צדקה complements משפט by its aspect of doing.

14:14 - נח דנאל ואיוב   Noah, Dn'l and Job

המה בצדקתם יצלו נפשם.   they will (only) save themselves by their just deeds.

The particle 'ב' in בצדקתם stands for 'by,' 'because of,' like בצדק in 18:22. The righteous person can only save himself at time of disaster, not even his (sinful) children, let alone his people.

In chapters 3, 14, 18 and 33 Ezekiel reiterates this idea which is summarized in 18:20:

18:20 - צדקת הצדיק עליו תהיה,   The good deeds of the righteous man shall be accounted to him (alone),

ורשעת (ה)רשע עליו תהיה.   and the evil deeds of the wicked man shall be accounted to him (alone).

Only in 3:20 צדק and צדקה appear together. It is an excellent example for the difference between the two words:

3:20 - ובשוב צדיק מצדקו...   If a righteous person turns away from his code of justice...

ולא תזכרן צדקתו אשר עשה.   all his good deeds that he did shall not be recorded.

18:24 - ובשוב צדיק מצדקתו ועשה עול...   If a righteous person turns away from his righteous deeds and does evil...

כל צדקתו אשר-עשה לא תזכרנה.   all his good deeds that he did shall not be recorded.

One may say that 3:20 is an error, to be emended to מצדקתו as in 18:24. But we find ביום שוב רשעו מרשעו and ביום שוב מרשעתו (33:12,18). צדק is a general term for adherence to the law. The phrase ובשוב צדיק מצדקו shows a state of being where a person pursued righteous deeds and for reasons unknown deviated from that state of being. צדקת are a person's numerous good deeds.

The terms צדקה and צדקת for Ezekiel are secular and religious human activity. צדקה is the state of being in which the righteous operate.

DEUTERO-ISAIAH

Here the discussion will be divided into two parts: the relation of צדקה to man and to God.

THE HUMAN צדקה

56:1a - שמרו משפט   Keep the law

ועשו צדקה.   and do what is right.

58:2 - כגוי אשר צדקה עשה   Like a people that does what is right

ומשפט אלהיו לא עזב.   and does not forsake the law of its God.

משפט and צדקה are human acts which can bring about God's צדקה and ישועה. Deutero-Isaiah provides several examples of what he means by saying משפט וצדקה: keeping the Sabbath, avoiding evil doing and keeping the covenant. Deutero-Isaiah uses משפט in the same way it is used in Exod. 21:1: ואלה המשפטים אשר תשים לפניהם 'These are the laws that you shall put before them.' One of these laws is keeping the Sabbath (Exod. 23:12).

In 56:2 the prophet describes the character of a person who will be saved in a general statement: ושמר ידו מעשות כל רע—'and stays his hand from doing any evil.' In other words, it is the person who does what is good and right, which is the meaning of צדקה. So again צדקה is associated with doing good deeds.

It also means to carry out God's will, as expressed later in v. 4: ובחרו באשר חפצתי—'those who chose what I desire.' What God wants should equate with what Israel wishes. משפט is specific: it is the law.

We see in both passages how Deutero-Isaiah introduces the idiom משפט וצדקה and then explains each term. As with Amos and Isaiah it is an idiom. He adds that they derive from the divine sphere. Later, in 58:5, he gives an example of what God wishes (יום רצון לה'—'an acceptable day to Adonai') against what the people wish (חפץ ביום תנצאו צבכם ביום הך—'on your fast day you see to your business'—v. 3).

Deutero-isaiah associates צדקה with doing (עשה) and with the knowledge of God

(דעת אלהים). Doing צדקה leads to God.

Israel has deviated from the law; her people practice only injustice. Even their

thoughts center on evil (59:2-8).

Ginsberg understands ישעה, צדקה and זרוע ('arm') as synonyms in the

meaning of 'divine vindication.'[37]

59:9 - על כן רחק משפט ממנו   That is why justice is far from us

ולא תשיגנו צדקה.   and the knowledge of God does not reach us.

59:14 - והסג אחור משפט   And so justice is turned back

וצדקה מרחוק תעמד.   and the knowledge of God stays afar.

54:14 - בצדקה תכונני.   You shall be established with the knowledge of God.

are two concepts through which one obtains peaceful life (v. 8).

They were both suspended, particularly צדקה which is the *knowledge of God*. This

knowledge and its implementation in life generate blessings to the people, because

they are divine and good. Doing evil keeps משפט וצדקה afar. צדקה is associated

with peace, truth and honesty (נכוח). In these passages צדקה is more specific than

'what is right.' It is דעת אלהים, which in 58:2 was only an element in the

knowledge of God. It is also connected with blessing.

In 54:14 צדקה is associated again with דעת אלהים (למודי ה') and peace (v. 13).

It will be the foundation on which Israel will be reestablished in her land. This

foundation is the knowledge of God itself.

46:12 - שמעו אלי אבירי לב,   Listen to me, you stout of heart,

הרחוקים מצדקה.   who are far from the knowledge of God.

In Ps. 76:6 אבירי לב are the valiant soldiers who are associated with chariots

and horses. In our passage they are not undaunted soldiers but morally deficient,

'stubborn of heart', who are far from צדקה, which is the source of strength in

society. That is the idea of Zechariah (4:6). Deutero-Isaiah shows that the spiritual strength is far more valuable and important in life than the physical prowess.

The heart symbolizes the center of thoughts. The prophet uses this symbol to mock those who think themselves to be mighty.

60:17 - ושמתי פקדתך שלום   I will appoint peace as your officers

ונגשיך צדקה.   and well-being as your magistrates.

Again צדקה is associated with peace, though its meaning changes. Before, צדקה would bring peace (59:8-9) and now it is *life where justice prevails*. Deutero-Isaiah's style as we recognized above returns but in a chiastic way: 'peace' is life where 'plunder and destruction in your borders' shall be no more; צדקה is life where 'violence shall no more be heard in your land.' חמס ('robbery') is a legal term for oppression, especially of the poor.

צדקה as 'well-being' or 'blessing' appears again in 48:18:

48:18 - ויהי כנהר שלומך   Your peace will be like a river

וצדקתך כגלי הים.   and your well-being like the waves of the sea.

Another chiastic style appears. Peace and צדקה are metaphorically portrayed as river and sea, which represent blessings (smooth, pure, abundant, peaceful). Now they are not tools but the end-result of good behavior. צדקה is a *state of peaceful living*.

48:1 - הנשבעים בשם ה'...יזכירו   Who swear by the name of Adonai...and invoke
                                      (His name)

לא באמת ולא בצדקה.   not in truth and not with right.

צדקה is associated with 'truth.' God accuses Israel of swearing by His name without sincerity. Only those who follow His teaching have this right, but since Israel worships idols (vv. 5b,8) this right has been revoked. This is very similar to Gen. 15:6 (where the verb אבץ appears with צדקה) and 2 Sam. 19:29. Jeremiah adds משפט (4:2). The context is the same: idolatry and swearing by God's name. Zechariah promises that God will return to Israel to be their God 'with truth and with right.'

Another interpretation may be suggested: Israel swears by God's name without being truthful and sincere, because they lack these values.

57:12 - אֲנִי אַגִּיד צִדְקָתֵךְ וְאֶת מַעֲשַׂיִךְ. I shall declare your deeds of rightness.

Rudolf Kittel wonders whether וְאֶת מַעֲשַׂיִךְ are a duplicate of צִדְקָתֵךְ and suggests that it may be an addition.[38] The suggestion is sound since צִדְקָתֵךְ involves deeds. It could originally be מַעֲשֵׂי צִדְקָתֵךְ or the intention was to parallel צִדְקָתֵךְ with מַעֲשַׂיִךְ. The idea is that Israel's deeds of rightness will not help when God pronounces judgment, for they are probably very few and meaningless. צְדָקָה is associated with an audible verb.

64:5 - וַנְּהִי כַטָּמֵא כֻּלָּנוּ We have all become like an unclean thing

וּכְבֶגֶד עִדִּים כָּל-צִדְקֹתֵינוּ. and all our good deeds like a filthy rag.

The word צִדְקֹתֵינוּ is the opposite of עִדִּים. Subsequently, צְדָקָה are the good deeds that are likened to unclean garments. 'Wearing' good deeds is like wearing clean clothes. It is a personal responsibility and moral statement. Whatever good deeds Israel performed she has defiled them, and at the same times defiled herself. Israel accepts her responsibility and confesses guilt.

In 54:17 צְדָקָה carries another nuance:

54:17 - זֹאת נַחֲלַת עַבְדֵי ה' Such is the lot of the servants of Adonai

וְצִדְקָתָם מֵאִתִּי. and their good fortune from Me.

Whatever will be plotted against Israel (any war machine or legal accusation), the prophet asserts, will be thwarted by God. This good fortune (i.e. victories) will be Israel's heritage.

The same idea is found in 45:24-25:

45:24 - אַךְ בַּה' לִי אָמַר צְדָקוֹת וָעֹז... Only through Adonai can I find good
fortune/victory and might...

v. 25 - בַּה' יִצְדְּקוּ וְיִתְהַלְלוּ כָּל זֶרַע יִשְׂרָאֵל. It is through Adonai that all the offspring
of Israel will find vindication and glory.

Only God is the source for good fortune and strength.

THE DIVINE צדקה

45:23 - בִּי נִשְׁבַּעְתִּי, יָצָא מִפִּי צְדָקָה,   By Myself have I sworn, from My mouth has
                                                                    issued vindication,

דָּבָר וְלֹא יָשׁוּב.   a pronouncement that will not turn back.

Dahood emends the first colon as follows: יָצָא מִפִּי צֶדֶק, הַדָּבָר וְלֹא יָשׁוּב.[39] I
agree with the reading of צֶדֶק which I explain as 'just verdict' (vindication) as in
62:1,2, Ps. 17:15, 37:6 and 40:10. However, I emend that phrase further, reading:

יָצָא מִפִּי צֶדֶק,

הַדִּבֵּר וְלֹא יָשׁוּב.

The word דִּבֵּר means 'word,' 'pronouncement' which parallels well with
צֶדֶק–'verdict.' It is in pi'el as תְּדַבֵּרוּן in Ps. 58:2a. In Ps. 51:6 we find a similar
form לְמַעַן תִּצְדַּק בְּדָבְרְךָ תִּזְכֶּה בְשָׁפְטֶךָ which I emend to לְמַעַן תִּצְדַּק בְּדַבֶּרְךָ, using
the pi'el and hence the reading: 'so you are right when you pronounce the just
verdict.' The verb דבר parallels שפט as in Ps. 58:2.[40] Furthermore, the reading of
צֶדֶק is preferred to צְדָקָה because it follows a masculine form (יָצָא). God vows that
His just verdict will not be altered.

If צְדָקָה is original, it would mean 'utterance' or 'decision.' It may be that this
צְדָקָה is the divine good decision: that every person will vow by Adonai; or that
good fortune will befall Israel. The meaning of 'utterance' for צְדָקָה is not attested
anywhere else.

In the next passages צְדָקָה not only comes directly from God, but is strongly
associated with the verb ישע ('to save') and its nouns יֵשַׁע, ישועה or תשועה.

45:8b - תִּפְתַּח-אֶרֶץ וְיִפְרוּ-יֶשַׁע,   Let the earth open up and salvation sprout,

וּצְדָקָה תַצְמִיחַ יַחַד.   and let blessing come forth too.

The imagery of blessing through rain and fertility of land is common as we
saw above. It is very similar to Hos. 10:12 where in both cases צֶדֶק and צְדָקָה
appear in the same verse, but in the reverse order. This may be a clue to the
dependency of Isa. 45:8 on Hos. 10:12. The same idea is expressed by Joel in

2:23. It is an old idea carried by the prophets and the Deuteronomist.

The syntax and grammar of the verse are confused: if יֵשַׁע is the result of the fertility of the earth (אֶרֶץ), then יִפְרֶה ('will sprout') should be emended to תַּפְרֶה. Consequently, יֵשַׁע will parallel צְדָקָה. Another possibility is that יֵשַׁע וּצְדָקָה constitute an idiom and they are not parallels: תִּפְתַּח-אֶרֶץ וְתִפְרֶה יֵשַׁע וּצְדָקָה—let the earth open up and bring forth salvation and blessing.' It is possible that the form יִפְרֶה follows the pattern of יִזַּל in v. 8a, which will then be a scribal error.

If יִפְרֶה is correct, then יֵשַׁע וּצְדָקָה should be in the same colon, to which יַחַד will refers, and the word תַצְמִיחַ will be deleted. The reading will be: וְיִפְרֶה יֵשַׁע וּצְדָקָה יַחַד(וֹ).

Another reading, based on the various possibilities, is this:

תִּפְתַּח אֶרֶץ   Let the earth open up

וְתִפְרֶה יֵשַׁע וּצְדָקָה יַחַד(וֹ),   and let her sprout salvation and blessing in unity

אֲנִי ה' בְּרָאתִים.   I, Adonai, have created them.

The skies open up and drip rain of blessing to the earth, which receives the rain in order to produce salvation and blessing. What we have here is a sharp distinction between צֶדֶק and צְדָקָה: צֶדֶק is a direct blessing from God. It is the incentive, the necessary ingredient to produce an earthly blessing—צְדָקָה. When the heavenly צֶדֶק reaches man it causes a secular, human kind of blessing, which is צְדָקָה.[41]

What is צְדָקָה? There may be two possibilities:

1.   It is the produce of the fertile land, namely, blessed crops.

2.   It refers to blessings of life in general: peace, prosperity, security, in short, personal and national blessings. The latter is more acceptable since the produce is יֵשַׁע and not a real crop. We are dealing with imagery and metaphors where צֶדֶק is a general term for a blessing and צְדָקָה is the actual, detailed blessings in active form.

The prophet does not explain in our verse what צְדָקָה comprises and it is left for us to fill the void. The Wisdom idea of צדקה may shed light on the prophetic term which is *the good life*. Proverbs also uses צדקה in agricultural imagery (11:18,30). ישע refers to inner salvation, of the individual and/or the nations: salvation from the maladies of society and not from outside enemies.

Most commentators contend that victory (ישע) and righteousness (צדקה) are identified with the conquests of Cyrus. These conquests are God's will and achievements.[42]

Closer to our suggestion is that of North, who translates צדקה as 'prosperity.'[43]

46:13 - קרבתי צדקתי לא תרחק   I am bringing My (active) grandeur close; it is not far

וישעתי לא תאחר.   and My salvation will not tarry.

ונתתי בציון תשועה,   And I will grant Zion salvation,

לישראל תפארתי.   to Israel My magnificence.

Deutero-Isaiah's style recognized above is repeated here in a chiastic form: ישעתי parallels תשועה and צדקתי parallels תפארתי. Usually תפארת is translated as 'glory,' 'pride,' 'honor.' Deutero-Isaiah plays on the word צדקה: in v. 12 it refers to the knowledge of God, and in v. 13—to the respectability and glory of God, which are associated with salvation or victory. The salvation and glory of God will change the present situation in which Israel sins against His (vv. 5-8). Israel is in a shameful state of idolatry. When salvation comes to cleanse her (when victory over idolatry will be established), God's glory will be passed on to her for possession. Only after Israel is cleansed will she be given a divine blessing in the form of a clean name and self-respect. צדקה and תשועה again are not synonymous.

Luzzatto raises an interesting point: תפארתי is a descriptive name for Israel and not a parallel to תשועה, just as ציון does not parallel ישראל. ציון parallels ירושלם, and ישראל–יעקב.[44]

Basically, his assumption is correct. However, the prophet says that victory will come to the *land* of Zion and respectability—to her *people* Israel. That is the reason for saying בְּצִיּוֹן and לְיִשְׂרָאֵל. The particle 'ב' points to a place, the particle 'ל' points to people.[45]

56:1b - כִּי קְרוֹבָה יְשׁוּעָתִי לָבֹא   For soon My salvation shall come

וְצִדְקָתִי לְהִגָּלוֹת.   and My (active) grandeur be revealed.

The same idea appears in 46:13. Also similar is the way the prophet uses both human and divine צדקה in the same breath. These two attributes (salvation and grandeur) will be an active force of change when they are revealed. Here the change refers to social injustice (v. 1a) as part of the overall adherence to the covenant (v. 4). The glory of God is like a good name, an eternal monument (v. 5. See also 63:14, Jer. 13:11, 33:9). Part of this change of state is the change of name or reputation. It is connected with the prophetic idea of name change, an idea which appears in passages like 1:26: אַחֲרֵי כֵן יִקָּרֵא לָךְ ('after that you shall be called'), 47:1,5: כִּי לֹא תוֹסִיפִי יִקְרְאוּ לָךְ ('nevermore shall they call you'), and 61:3: וְקֹרָא לָהֶם...לְהִתְפָּאֵר ('they shall be called...to be glorified').

Deutero-Isaiah (or Third Isaiah?) uses צדק and כבוד ('honor' - 62:1-2) in the same way as צדקה and תפארה ('glory' - 56:13), but the meaning of צדק there is 'vindication.' Furthermore, יְשׁוּעָה, צדק and כבוד are connected (also 58:8, 51:5). In 46:13 they are צדקה, תשועה and תפארה. This choice of words seems to be intentional and significant. יְשׁוּעָה, צדק and כבוד are all masculine words while תשועה, צדקה and תפארה are feminine forms.[46] Since כבוד has no feminine form, תפארה takes its place.

51:6 - וִישׁוּעָתִי לְעוֹלָם תִּהְיֶה   My salvation shall stand forever

וְצִדְקָתִי לֹא תֵחָת.   and My (active) grandeur shall remain unbroken.

51:8 - וְצִדְקָתִי לְעוֹלָם תִּהְיֶה   My (active) grandeur shall stand forever

וִישׁוּעָתִי לְדוֹר דּוֹרִים.   and My salvation through all the ages.

What emanates of God is perpetual, in contrast to man's life. Furthermore, it is not only a statement of the eternity of God's salvation and magnificence, but a reassurance that these attributes are there to be active. When He decides to reveal

His ישועה and צדקה, they will immediately be activated. The phrase לא תחת is synonymous with לחד דורים in the meaning of 'steadfast,' 'invincible,' 'indestructible' (Jer. 14:4, 1 Sam. 2:4).[47]

59:16 - ותושע לו זרעו,   His own arm won Him triumph,

וצדקתו היא סמכתהו.   and His (active) grandeur supported Him.

The passage discusses the lack of justice in the society, where sins are many. No one intervenes to save this society, until God Himself comes forth to take action. He calls upon His arm and His active grandeur to carry out justice. The arm is a symbol for might, and the grandeur is a symbol for the active ingredient in that might, the force behind the arm.

Similarly is 63:5 where instead of צדקתו there comes חמתי ('My anger'). The divine anger is described as the divine weapon to punish the nations. The anger is powerful just like the arm and the divine grandeur. צדקה and חֵמָה are forces in action. Are they one and the same or two forces in one, analogous to two sides of a coin? Probably the latter.

Rosenberg deduces from this connection that צדקה means 'vengeance.' However, right before this he says that צדקה supports God in His vengeance against His enemies.[48]

59:17 - וילבש צדקה כשרין   He wore (active) grandeur as a coat of mail

וכובע ישועה בראשו.   and a helmet of salvation on His head.

God appears as a warrior, putting on His weapons, ready for action. The abstract terms become real. They can be seen as war garments. שם ה' ('Adonai's name') and His כבוד will be feared by all (v. 19). These are the divine צדקה: His magnitude, His true fame and grandeur. Wearing צדקה is taking up responsibility to help the needy.

61:10 - כי הלבישני בגדי-ישע,   For He has clothed me with garments of salvation,

מעיל צדקה יעטני.   wrapped me in a robe of well-being/purity.

The same clothes, after saving Israel, were given as a token of cleansing and completion of act, to Israel. Now her purity is exposed to all. Israel is compare to

a bridegroom who wears beautiful clothes (פאר). The war garments have been

changed into garments of peace and happiness. צדקה becomes a state of well-being,

of joy.[49]

Whenever ישע and צדקה appear together, the usual interpretation is that God's

righteousness is manifested through salvation (Gordon, Bollier, Olley and many

others). This idea is deduced because צדקה and ישע appear in parallel. The

scholars do not go beyond this. If they parallel, they argue, either they mean the

same or one depends upon the other. But parallels have more functions. זרוע ('arm')

is not חמה ('anger' - 63:5b), עניה ('poor') is not שכרה ('drunk' - 51:21), משפט

('judgment,' 'equity') is not פעולה ('action' - 49:5b). The idea behind the parallels

needs to be sought. Sometimes there is an associative link, or simply an idiom of

the time, e.g. צמח וצדקה ,צדקה ותהלה, that occasionally is parted to create

parallelism.

61:11 - אדני אלהים יצמיח צדקה ותהלה   Adonai Elohim will make (His active)

grandeur and praise sprout

נגד כל-הגוים.   before all nations.

Again צדקה is used in the form of an agricultural metaphor. God causes things

to happen. Here, too, He will cause His glory and praise to grow,[50] as a natural

result of the renewal of the covenant with His people (v. 8). The blessing upon

Israel among the nations (v. 9) will reflect upon His glory and magnitude.

63:1 - אני מדבר בצדקה,   It is I who speak through (My active) grandeur,

רב להושיע.   powerful to grant salvation.

The function of the particle 'ב' is similar to that of 'ב' in 1:27, 5:26, 54:14

and Prov. 16:12. צדקה is portrayed here as a positive force. 'Force' is supported

by רב כחו ('his great might') that precede it. The word רב refers to a person while

the word רב that follows refers to God, and כחו, which refers to a person, is

transferred to the divine sphere through צדקה. The word of God takes on action through His attribute of magnificence.

Some commentators feel that 'righteousness' does not fit the context and therefore suggest other translations: 'vindication' (Kraeling), 'truth' (Wade), 'fidelity' (Leslie), 'in the manner of saving' (Olley). Cheyne explains that the prophet wants to depict God as mighty in word as in act. צדקה means "the fidelity of God to His revealed principles of action."[51]

ZECHARIAH

The word צדקה appears only once in Zechariah.

8:8 - והיו לי לעם   And they shall be My people

ואני אהיה להם לאלהים   and I will be their God

באמת ובצדקה.   in truth and with right.

Zechariah probably bases his prophecy on Deutero-Isaiah (48:2). There the prophet refers to the sinful people who vow by the name of God with no truth in their heart and with no right to do so. These are the hypocrites. Zechariah refers to that generation of הימים הראשנים—the former days—who did not deserve the divine blessings (vv. 11-13). The returning remnant deserves a new relationship. This time God will establish a new covenant rightfully and truthfully, because both parties will be reliable and sincere.

Zechariah counters and invalidates Deutero-Isaiah's negativity. He assures his community that they will inherit the blessings which the former prophets had promised to the remnant (e.g. Isa. 32:18, Jer. 4:2). If the phrase באמת ובצדקה refers to people, then בצדקה will be a state of being in which they act righteously and rightly, either with one another or with God (vv. 16-17). It would have the same meaning as Ezekiel's צדקה.

Emery Barnes explains that God "will be true to His people and perform acts of righteousness for them" and conversely they will be true to God and to their fellow man.[52]

Mitchell explains this 'righteousness' as being truthful and steadfast to the requirements of the new relation, either by God or by man.[53]

According to Mordechai Zer-Kavod באמת ובצדקה refer to ישבו. The people are restored in Jerusalem by right of their deeds of truth and justice.[54] צדקה does not refer then to the new covenant.

MALACHI

The word צדקה appears twice in Malachi.

3:3 - .והיו לה' מגישי מנחה בצדקה   And they shall present offerings to Adonai with right (rightfully).

The priests, the Sons of Levi, are accused of having been careless in the conduct of the sacrifices (1:6-2:9). By breaching the "covenant of Levi" (2:8) they have abrogated their right to their office. However, God will not annul their priesthood, He will purify them. Only then will their right to offer sacrifices to God be restored.

P. M. Smith explains בצדקה as "in accordance with all the requirements of the ritual,"[55] the way Mitchell interpreted it. As Zechariah, Deutero-Isaiah and Jeremiah, Malachi talks about a new covenant that will be established on more truthful and secure grounds.

Rex Mason's translation is different than others. בצדקה, he says, means "they shall be fit."[56] Zer-Kavod, true to his previous explanation, says that בצדקה means "by their deeds of justice."[57]

Kimhi and Metzudat Zion explain בצדקה 'According to the sacrificial laws,' 'appropriately'[58] as against the unlawful practices done now (1:7-8,12-14, 2:11-12).

3:20 - וזרחה לכם, יראי שמי   But for you, who revere My name,

שמש צדקה ומרפא בכנפיה.   a sun of blessing shall rise with healing in its wings.

Here צדקה can mean 'blessing,' 'goodness,' 'soothing,' 'benevolence' against כל עשה רשעה ('all the doers of evil'—v. 19) and their awful end, which is compared to a burning day. The sun will not burn the righteous but heal them through warmth and blessing.

The idea of goodness coming from the sun is associated with God in Ps. 84:12. This psalm is a Wisdom composition which may point to its influence on Malachi. יראי שמי are those צדיקים in the Wisdom literature and צדקה is the blessing of heaven over them. This blessing comprises prosperity, security and especially good health (if we take מרפא literally). The figure of שמש צדקה is similar to צדקה צמח, where צדקה was explained as an adjective the way it is here.

Smith maintains that on that day God's "righteousness (will) illumine the gloom of Israel's afflictions." The sun itself, represented by the Babylonian Shamash, is the manifestation of justice. The metaphor of שמש צדקה is "a figurative representation of righteousness itself." צדקה, righteousness, is "practically equivalent to vindication and victory as (it) is so often in Deutero-Isaiah."[59] Zer-Kavod interprets similarly: 'a day of salvation.'[60]

Gordon interprets שמש צדקה as the light and warmth of the divine salvation.[61] God, says Mason, is depicted like the rising sun after the night of distress, to help the righteous. He comes to establish righteousness.[62]

DANIEL

The word צדקה appears three times, all in Daniel's prayer.

9:7 - לך ה' הצדקה   To you, Adonai, rightness

ולנו בשת הפנים.   and to us—disgrace.

Daniel's style is similar to that of Deutero-Isaiah. He makes a statement made of two parts. Then he explains each part in a reversed order: why is disgrace our lot? Because we have sinned. Why is צדקה God's lot? Because He is all compassion and pardon (vv. 8-9). The state of being in shame is in contrast with the state of being in the right. God has been true to His commitment to Israel,[63] but Israel failed and suffered the consequences. God was in the right all the time. This is expressed also in Lam. 1:18 and in Neh. 9:33.

Heaton defines צדקה as rightness, the very essence of God's nature.[64] Similar is Russell's explanation: "He is righteous in the sense that He always acts in conformity with His own character."[65] André Lacoque links this conformity with the covenant.[66]

9:16 - ה' בכל צדקתיך   Adonai, as befits all Your right (righteous) deeds

ישב-נא אפך וחמתך.   let Your anger and wrath turn away.

Daniel mentions a number of God's deeds to Israel which include good deeds and periods of punishment throughout her history. All these were right acts according to His teaching and His Torah (vv. 10-11). He is still צדיק for all He has done (v. 14). All His historical activities are His צדקה, divine acts done rightly. As He declared through His prophets, there will come a new era, an era of peace and prosperity. Daniel calls for God to bring about this era through that same power. This power (צדקת) can cause good and bad acts and always is in the right. This is not the exclusive saving acts of God as expressed by Deutero-Isaiah. Daniel's צדקה has a destructive, punitive side too.

The translation 'acts of vindication' (James Montgomery, Louis Hartman) does not convey the dual function of the divine צדק. 'Righteous acts' (Norman Porteus, Russell) would be more appropriate, but not 'goodness.'[67]

9:18 - כי לא על צדקתינו   For not because of any right (rightness) deeds of ours

אנחנו מפילים תחנונינו לפניך.   do we lay our supplications before You.

In this verse צדקה refers to the human right deeds. Daniel, speaking for the whole nation, confesses that Israel can count on a few deeds as merits, but they do not weigh enough to bring about a change for the better. They can only rely on God's compassion. The change will take place for the sake of God's name and essence (vv. 17,19, Jer. 14:7, Ezek. 20:44, Isa. 48:9,11). They are the צדקה that Jeremiah (51:10), Ezekiel (3:20, 18:24) and Deutero-isaiah (64:5) talked about. Also, the Aramaic צִדְקָה (4:24) has the same meaning as its plural form: a good, right deed.

Daniel uses צדקה for God and for man alike but there is a great difference:

when it relates to man צדקה is simply a good deed; God's acts in the plural form
of צדקות are always right, even when they cause destruction. Whatever He does
is right.

Hartman senses the difference between both צדקה and translates here 'merits,'
explaining them literally as righteous acts, good deeds.

Summary: The word צדקה in the prophets is used in a variety of meanings.
First and foremost, it is a divine source given to man in order to create a balanced,
healthy society. It is God's positive power that saves Israel, that changes historical
events for His sake. This power is His blessing that results in peaceful living, in
prosperity, abundance of goodness, strength, salvation, Wisdom and in the
knowledge of God. צדקה for Isaiah, Amos and Hosea, is the means to get these
blessings. The means is living by the law and doing good deeds. It is a *code of
behavior.*

צדקה relates to two aspects: social justice and being faithful to God (Isaiah,
Jeremiah, Ezekiel). צדק and משפט belong only to the legal aspect. Ezekiel is the
first prophet to synthesize both religious and social aspects in the idiom משפט
וצדקה. Amos, who relates צדקה to legal matters, also talks about צדקה in terms of
acts of benevolence and kindness. For Jeremiah, knowing God leads to doing what
is right. The result is peaceful and secure life. He also connects צדקה with the
function of the king. This will result in securing his dynasty.

Deutero-Isaiah developed צדקה to its highest stage. He employs it in all the
ways his predecessors did. What was only a means to reach the knowledge of God
has become this knowledge itself. Doing evil keeps it away, so the blessings are
suspended. He equates the divine with the human צדקה to underline their
interdependency.

It is spiritual as well as an actual state of life where peace, truth and honesty
dwell. It is the source of strength of the society. It brings peace and at the same
time it is peace itself. While צדק is what God sends down from heaven, צדקה is

צדקה in the Prophets   137

its implementation on earth.

It is power that mostly comes to bless. Deutero-Isaiah attributes this power to a new concept: the divine grandeur. It is the active part of that power which results in salvation, which in turn cleanses Israel from idolatry. Then this grandeur will be kept by Israel for possession.

צדקה is also the good fortune (i.e. divine blessing) that is Israel's heritage.

משפט וצדקה is an idiom that relates to the moral conduct and acts of man in accordance with the law. It includes secular and religious aspects of the law.

צדקה is compared to water that brings blessings (Amos, Joel, Isaiah, Deutero-Isaiah) and to a healing sun (Malachi). Hosea, Isaiah, Amos, Joel, Jeremiah and Deutero-Isaiah illustrate the divine צדקה in agricultural terms. Speaking the truth, another meaning for צדקה, is compared by Isaiah to walking on a straight path.

The post-exilic prophets (and perhaps Jeremiah) employ צדקה as 'right,' 'merit,' the way it appears in the narrative literature. It is more evident in this late period than in the pre-exilic period.

In a number of cases it seems that צדקה is preferred to צדק (or vice versa) for merely poetic considerations. It is mostly evident when they appear in the same verse or unit to create puns.

TABLE 7

Book	Good deeds of man	Good deeds of king	Righteousness of God	Divine saving acts	Divine blessing	Innocence, vindication
Isa.	8	1	1	–	1	1(?)
Hos.	–	–	–	–	1	–
Amos	3	–	–	–	–	–
Micah	–	–	–	1	–	1
Joel	–	–	–	–	1	–
Jer.	3	2	1	–	–	1
Ezek.	20	–	–	–	–	–
Deut.-Isa.	4	–	–	8*	1	1
Mal.	–	–	–	–	1	–
Dan.	1	–	1	1	–	–

Book	Divine active grandeur	knowledge of God	Good fortune	Right, merit	Being faithful	Well-being
Isa.	–	–	–	–	1	–
Jer.	–	–	–	–	1	–
Deut.-Isa.	8	4	2	1	–	3
Zech.	–	–	–	1	–	–
Mal.	–	–	–	1	–	–

* For Deutero-Isaiah *divine active grandeur* and *divine saving acts* are closely connected.

9

צִדְקוֹת ה'

The early song of Deborah (Judg. 5) and probably the Blessing of Moses (Deut. 33) illustrate the original meaning of the phrase צִדְקוֹת ה'. In Judg. 5:11 and Deut. 33:21 it means the war victories of Israel that were regarded as God's active intervention on behalf of His chosen people. These stories were told by the warriors at tribal meetings and later became part of the orally transmitted folklore history and literature. Past tribal and national events became the social matter that identified the individual with his people. When the tribe Gad carried out God's צדקה, it meant that he fought Israel's wars as God's messenger. He fulfilled God's will and plan by protecting Israel and at the same time by living up to His rules (מִשְׁפָּטִים). Gad conformed with Israel's destiny and life although he lived east of the Jordan river.

Originally, צִדְקוֹת ה' were composed as songs of victories before and especially after battle. In Judg. 4 we find the narrative version of Deborah's song in the next chapter. These songs of victories, claims Norman K. Gottwald, were put on the lips of women representing the mothers of Israel. In the case of Hannah, elements originally applied to the people Israel, were made available to the individual believer.

The function of these songs, continues Gottwald, was to preserve the separate tribal identities, which were fitted into the centralized cult in times of celebrations. According to his theory, the nation of Israel started out from diverse Semitic groups of Canaanites and groups who left Egypt, bringing with them the Sinai and

Yahwistic traditions. What amalgamated these assorted groups was the Yahwistic cult, which was unique and innovative. In this cult, the songs of victory or the songs of salvation constituted a profound role in the creation of the new union. They were the "foundation story of United Israel." The saving acts tradition was a social means in reinforcing the ideological unity of Israel.

The victories of the theophany were an expression of god's sovereignty in Israel, and a focal point for the creation of a theophanic cult, a cult of vital importance before and after warfare. Tribal wars were conceived as the war of the whole nation. The tribal songs of salvation, depicting God as the protector and intervener on Israel's behalf, found their way into the Passover-festival theme and from there to the theme of Deliverance from Egypt.[1]

Leonard Thompson suggests that צדקת ה', in a narrative form, is what we would call today 'a myth': they are the mythic transformation of Israel from a state of chaos to a state of order. They are god's manifestation as the sustainer of order. Their recitation was essential in order to maintain Israel's social order.[2]

When one tells of צדקת ה' he recounts God's deeds in protecting the individual or the nation. There is a strong faith and trust that God will come again to secure the safety of His believer or His people. Past victories against odds were the psychological as well as the nationalistic safety valve upon which the people relied.

צדקת ה' maintained their meaning during the period of the monarchy (1. Sam. 12:7, Micah 6:5, Ps. 103:3). They were identified with תהלות (songs of glory and praise). The prophets saw them as the building material for stability, continuity, order, harmony and national pride. God's acts were an integral part of reality, of life itself.

Since the saving acts of God were good, צדקת ה' became a term for any good, right act of God (Isa. 33:15). Deutero-Isaiah added to צדקת a sense of 'active force', that emanates from His glory and magnificence (45:24).

Daniel brought this term to its latest development. God's צדקת are always right and good whether they are benevolent or destructive in nature (9:16).

10

CONCLUSIONS

The main observations from this study are the following:

1. צדק stands, in most cases, as a general term for 'justice,' 'rightness,' 'righteousness' and 'blessing.' צדקה is broader in meaning and is more specific than צדק. It is a *state of being*, human and divine. It is self-fulfillment according to the ultimate *code of ethics*. It is a set of behavior and actions.[1]

Hebrew recognizes masculine and feminine forms of צדק because they convey different meanings. It is definitely not a matter of caprice, except for some cases in poetry when the poet needs to create special rhymes and effect to transmit to his listeners.

צדק and צדקה are concepts in terms of relationships: between man and man according to the customs of society, and between man and God according to a special covenant. The laws of this covenant must be maintained as complementary to the local customs.

There is no evidence that צדקה in the Bible has the meaning of 'charity,' 'almsgiving,' as several scholars claim. It is a post-Biblical development from the aramaic.

2. All genres of literature make a distinction between צדק and צדקה.

a. In the Narrative צדק is exclusively a nomistic term. צדקה is the proper behavior and acts of man. It may also refer to the essence of God.

b. In the Wisdom literature צדק is strongly connected with the judicial procedures in court and with the rightness of man and king (the human domain).

Psalms uses צדק as the righteousness of God and as a protective element mainly in legal matters. צדקה refers to both the righteous deeds of man and those of God. However, the divine צדקה has taken a different route. It is the glorious, wondrous acts of God in nature, in the universe, and to Israel and the individual. This stems from His goodness.

It is also the *blessed protective sphere* that is kept for those who do righteous acts (צדקה in double meaning). It is cause and effect. It is a worldly blessing.

For Wisdom צדקה is a way of life. It is a philosophy.

צדקה, as a legal term, either in the human or in the divine sphere, is completely absent. It is ethical in nature in both spheres.

c. In the Prophets צדק is connected with nomistic matters, with rightness of man/king and God alike. However, Deutero-Isaiah employs it as the divine attribute of justice. For Ezekiel it has only a human application: legal and the overall just conduct of man.[2]

צדקה varies from Isaiah to Daniel. We see a gradual development: for Isaiah it is the good acts of man and God. The difference is almost indistinguishable. For Amos and Ezekiel it is only the good deeds of man. Jeremiah associates it with the king's duty as keeper of the law and customs. Deutero-Isaiah uses the meanings of his predecessors but adds new ones. He develops the idea of צדקה as the glorious acts of God, into His active grandeur (כבוד, תפארת). This power is that which protects God's people in order to glorify and validate His own name among the nations. It is the power that bestows good fortune upon His chosen ones. It is peace itself. Daniel employs the three main meanings of the word: good deeds of man and of God, and His glorious acts of protection.

3.   Throughout the literature צדק is closely related to what is straight, right and true in *legal* matters. It is a general term for *what is right* (as noun and as adjective) in the human and divine spheres. It is the basis on which a king should establish his throne.

4. In all the literature צדקה relates to actions according to the divine code of ethics. Subsequently, it became the *rewards* that God gives to man directly or through the blessing of the land. These rewards and blessings take the form of agricultural benefits. This is evident in the Prophets (Isaiah, Hosea, Joel, Amos, Jeremiah and Deutero-Isaiah) and in Proverbs.

The relationship between God and Israel is symbolized by the relationship between man and his land. The idea of rewards probably originated in the Wisdom circle and passed on to the prophets and the Deuteronomistic school.[3]

The influence of Wisdom on the prophets was immense in ideas, terminology and style. צדקה has gone beyond the divine attribute of righteousness. It has been identified with God's power to cause changes in the world, to control historical events, to change nature, to protect and to bless or to cause disasters. All that stems from His צדקה, His righteousness. This blessing brings harmony, abundance, happiness, peace, security, prosperity, honor and longevity.

צדקה is a *state of being*. In Wisdom its power protects the individual; in the Prophets it protects the people Israel.

5. In all the literature and throughout the Biblical period צדקה as 'right,' 'merit' persisted, from Samuel through Psalms, to Malachi, Zechariah and Nehemiah. However, while in Samuel this merit was granted according to local customs, later it meant the right according to the divine laws.

6. In the Prophets צדקה may also mean 'innocence' and 'vindication.'[4] However, Psalms and Deutero-Isaiah use צדק for this meaning as well.

7. Based upon the idea of 'rewards' Deutero-Isaiah introduced his theory of the correlation between צדקה and salvation. When the righteousness of God goes into action it results in salvation.

8. At the basis of all the literature צדק and צדקה are the ultimate code, the divine criterion of what is right. The prophets underline one aspect or the other. Isaiah emphasizes the legal aspect of צדק while Zechariah emphasizes its ethical aspect.

Hosea, Joel and Deutero-Isaiah underline the aspect of blessing. They show interdependency on each other. They associate צדק with the knowledge/way/teaching of God. It may be knowledge itself or the goal to pursue it.

For Deutero-Isaiah צדק is learnt through Torah. Salvation is acquired through צדק. For Jeremiah צדק is part of God's name. While in Psalms צדק is a divine quality, in Jeremiah it describes the divine essence.

9. In Priestly and Prophetic literature צדק and holiness are strongly linked. Who may have influence whom is difficult to determine. For both, the divine holiness and justice are interconnected. However, Deutero-Isaiah polarizes these two groups: the Priestly theology maintains that Israel's holiness is guaranteed by God's holiness and by צדק. Deutero-Isaiah maintains that Israel's well-being guarantees the credibility of God's holiness and צדק among the nations. The difference is profound.

10. Wisdom and the Prophets go beyond the basic meaning of the root צדק, 'straight' (still connected by Wisdom, Psalms, Isaiah, Ezekiel and Deutero-Isaiah), and give it legal and ethical meanings. Deutero-Isaiah brings צדק to its apex. The connection with 'straight' fades away toward the 4th century BCE. Today this meaning is nonexistent.

11. The image of צדק as a garment may have a development through the years: Isaiah sees the king as wearing צדק while the psalmist uses this imagery for the priests, and Deutero-Isaiah—for all Israel.

12. Isaiah, Jeremiah, Deutero-Isaiah and Daniel look forward to the time when God's צדק will reign on earth. Then, there will arise new conditions: a new covenant, a new vow, a new sense of justice and new names.

13. While Wisdom underlines the rightness of man, the prophets and the psalmists underline the righteousness of God. Wisdom is interested more in life situations, while the others are interested in the right relationship between man and God.

14. Most of the texts employ צדק as an adjective and some employ it as an adverb (Narrative, Psalms, Isaiah and Deutero-Isaiah).

15. Wisdom, Psalms and the Prophets extract צדק from its legal connection to be associated with any situation in life. While Wisdom regards it as a component of the 'good path' that leads to understanding the divine essence and to be closer to Him, the psalmists and most of the prophets elevate it all the way to the divine sphere. The pursuit of this צדק enables the righteous to apply it to their life. צדק has made a complete circle.

16. Among the prophets there are some differences in their use of the terms: Isaiah's צדק is the attribute of the king's justice. Jeremiah uses צדקה. Hosea's צדקה, taken up by Isaiah, Joel and Deutero-Isaiah, is an allegory for 'blessing.' The Deuteronomist makes it real.[5] This idea is further developed by Deutero-Isaiah: what צדק meant for Hosea, Isaiah and Zephaniah (the way to reach God's knowledge), is now צדקה for Deutero-Isaiah which has taken on the meaning of knowledge itself.

17. Two idioms are identified: צדק/ה ומשפט and משפט וצדק/ה. The former relates by and large to anyone in any situation. Ethical behavior and acts are emphasized. The latter relates mainly to the king and the judges where adherence to the law takes precedence. A good king, who fears his God, establishes his rule on משפט וצדק/ה.

Both idioms express the totality of what is just and ethical. It is especially so in משפט וצדקה where rightness in society cannot be established unless the law has been implemented. It is strongly evident in Ezekiel and the Narrative, where court justice is primarily emphasized. צדק/ה ומשפט, the general ethical behavior, are emphasized primarily in Wisdom.

18. צדק is also what one utters. It is associated with verbs like דִּבֶּר ('to speak'), קָרָא ('to call'), הָגָה ('to utter'), הִגִּיד ('to proclaim'). When it is so צדק is connected with speech at court, like giving true evidence, presenting the case or

pronouncing just verdicts.

19. In poetry, in some cases, and mostly in late texts, the distinction between צדק
and צדקה disappears (see points 1 and 6). It is mostly so when both words appear
in the same verse or unit.[6]

20. צדק or צדקה as 'legitimate' is not attested in the Bible. The phrase צמח צדקה
relates only to the ethical quality of the king. 'Rightfully' may be one of the
meanings of the adverb בצדק (Ps. 17:15).

21. Both צדק and צדקה delineate the human and the divine spheres. The distinction
between the secular and the divine is very slim, for the laws and ethics emanate
from the one and only source.

TABLE 8

צֶדֶק AND צְדָקָה IN THE BIBLE

Book	צֶדֶק	צְדָקָה	Book	צֶדֶק	צְדָקָה
Genesis	–	3	Jeremiah	6	8
Leviticus	5	–	Ezekiel	4	20
Deuteronomy	7	5	Deut.-Isaiah	17	24
Judges	–	2	Malachi	–	2
Samuel	–	6	Zechariah	–	1
Kings	–	3	Nehemiah	–	1
Isaiah	8	12	Chronicles	–	3
Hosea	2	1	Daniel	1	3
Micah	–	2	Psalms	50	34
Amos	–	3	Proverbs	8	18
Joel	–	1	Job	7	4
Zephaniah	1	–	Qoheleth	3	–

Total: צֶדֶק - **119**

צְדָקָה - **156**

TABLE 9

צדק ACCORDING TO GENRES

Applied to Man	Narrative	Wisdom	Prophets
Legal	Exod., Lev., Deut.: The right criterion of a judge.	Ps., Prov., Job, Qoh.: Judicial procedures in court.	
Ethical		Ps., Prov., Job, Qoh.: Rightness of man; Ps. Prov.: Rightness of king.	Isa., Jer., Ezek., Deut.-Isa.: Rightness of man; Isa. Jer.: Rightness of king.

TABLE 9 (Continued)

צדק ACCORDING TO GENRES

Applied to God	Narrative	Wisdom	Prophets
Legal			Deut.-Isa.: Divine attribute of justice.
Ethical		Ps., Job: Divine righteousness.	Isa., Hos., Zeph., Jer., Deut.-Isa., Dan.: Divine rightness; Hos., Deut.-Isa.: Divine blessing.

TABLE 10

צְדָקָה ACCORDING TO GENRES

Applied to Man	Narrative	Wisdom	Prophets
Legal	Sam., Kgs., Chron.: Legal conduct of king; Sam.: Claim, merit, according to local customs; Ps.*, Neh.: claim according to divine laws.		Isa., Micah, Jer.: Innocence, vindication.
Ethical	Gen.: Proper behavior and actions according to local customs; Gen. Deut., Sam., Kgs.: Proper behavior and actions according to divine laws.	Ps., Prov., Job: Proper behavior and actions; Job: Social integrity.	Isa., Amos, Jer., Ezek., Deut.-Isa.: Good deeds of man; Isa., Jer.: good deeds of king; Deut.-Isa.: Knowledge of God; Jer.(?), Deut.-Isa., Zech., Mal.: Merit, right; Isa., Jer., Ezek.: Being faithful; Deut.-Isa.: Well-being.

*In Ps. 106:31 צְדָקָה appears in a narrative style.

TABLE 10 (Continued)

צְדָקָה ACCORDING TO GENRES

Applied to God	Narrative	Wisdom	Prophets
Legal			
Ethical	Gen.: God's truthfulness to His promises; Deut.: Divine reward.	Ps.: Divine goodness and righteousness through wondrous acts.	Isa., Jer., Dan.: Divine righteousness; Micah, Deut.-Isa., Dan.: Divine saving acts; Isa., Hos., Joel, Mal.: Divine blessing; Deut.-Isa.: Divine grandeur.

TABLE 11

צֶדֶק AND צְדָקָה ACCORDING TO GENRES

Genre	צֶדֶק	צְדָקָה
Narrative	12	23
Wisdom	68	56
Prophets	39	77

ENDNOTES
INTRODUCTION

1. James Barr, *Comparative Philology and the Text of the Old Testament* (Oxford: Clarendon Press, 1968), 90, 157.

2. For example: time, place, vagueness in meaning, misunderstanding by the young generation; when a word is detached from its environment; when polysemy occurs; when contexts are ambiguous; when shifts occur in the structure of the vocabulary. Stephen Ullmann, *Semantics* (N.Y.: Barnes and Noble, 1962), 193-95. Languages change also as a result of metaphors.

3. Ullmann, 245-51.

4. E.g., in Job אַף means only 'not.' Barr, 147.

5. Barr, 90-91.

6. John F. Sawyer, *Semantics in Biblical Research* (in the series "Studies in Biblical Theology," 2/24, 1972), 92-93.

7. שלמה מורג, "שרי תרומות" (שמ"ב 21:1) ביטוי מחור", לשוננו, 45 (ניסן-תמוז תשמ"א):
318-317. See also Sawyer, 92-93.

8. יצחק אבישר, "וכליוחי אשותן (תה' 21:73) למשמעות הפועל שך בעברית ובאוגריתית."
לשוננו 44 (4) (תמוז תש"מ): 267-263.

9. John Sawyer, *A Modern Introduction to Biblical Hebrew* (Boston: Oriel Press, 1976), 163-71. These points are discussed in more detail in his book *Semantics in Biblical Research*; See also Barr, especially chapters I, II, IV-VII; Ullmann, 193ff. The rest of the examples are mine.

10. This is the method chosen by Eliezer Rubinstein, for example, when he examines the verbs שָׁלַח-שָׁלַח. He adds another method, that of the

syntactic structure of the sentence or phrase where variant roots appear.
אליעזר רובינשטין, "שֶׁלַח-שָׁלַח, עיון תחבירי וסמנטי בלשון המקרא," לשוננו 38
(תשל"א): 11-32.

11. Ullmann, 128.

12. Leonard Bloomfield, *Language* (N.Y.: H. Holt & Co., 1961), 145.

13. Ullmann, 128-54. In addition, W.E. Collinson outlines nine typical differences between synonyms in his book *Comparative Synonyms: Some Principles and Illustrations* (Transactions of the Philological Society, 1939), 61ff. Cited by Ullmann, 142-43.

14. Homonymy is sometimes mistaken as polysemy. The same method is used, though: support from other Semitic languages and extra-biblical literature. A good example can be found in Nahum M. Bronznik's article: "הסמנטיקה של השרש חל"ש להסתעפייותיו," לשוננו 41 (ניסן תשל"ז): 163-175.

15. זאב בן-חיים, "השרש ערב, הכלול ב' והנלוה עמו," לשוננו 44 (טבת תש"מ): 85-99.

16. E.g., *'oth, balah, bayith, baśar, gabhar, goy.*

17. Alexander To Ha Luc, *The Meaning of* אזב *in the Hebrew Bible,*" a Ph.D. dissertation at the University of Wisconsin-Madison, 1982.

18. J. Maxwell Miller, "In the "Image" and "Likeness" of God," *JBL* 91 (1972): 289-304.

19. In order to investigate the extension of meaning and stages of development of מטה ('staff', 'tribe') and שבט ('scepter,' 'tribe'), Ataliah Brenner suggests a number of semantic approaches. Before doing so she states the initial data: the original meaning and the final meaning. An intermediate link is missing in the development. The inquiry entails the following: the associative range, the semantic fields, their homonyms, synonyms, synchronic and diachronic relations. This is done through contextual research. As Luc, she too classifies her work according to meaning-content. Translations, cognate usages, dictionaries and commentaries (especially the traditional ones) are brought in

support for a point or suggestion. עתליה ברנר, "על מטה ושבט וסיחון וסוחן הסממי׳,"

לשוננו 44 (טבת תש"מ): 100-108.

20. John W. Olley, *"Righteousness" in the Septuagint of Isaiah: a Contextual Study* (Missoula, Montana: Scholars Press, 1979).

CHAPTER 1

1. Stanley A. Cook, *The Truth of the Bible* (London, 1938), 109.

2. Norman H. Snaith, *The Distinctive Ideas of the Old Testament* (London: The Epworth Press, 1944), 72. It seems more appropriate that the opposite of 'loose' is 'firm' rather than 'straight.'

3. Charles F. Whitley quotes E.W. Lane's *An Arabic-English Lexicon* (London, 1863-93), I, 4, p. 1667, col. 3, in his article "Deutero-Isaiah's Interpretation of Ṣedeq," *VT* 22 (October 1972): 469.

4. Edward F. Campbell, Jr. dates the six Jerusalem letters to about 1368-1351 BCE in "The Amarna Letters and the Amarna Period," *BA* 23 (February 1960): 10-11.

5. Letter no. 287, *ANET*, ed. James B. Prichard (Princeton: Princeton University Press, 1955), 488a.

6. Cyrus H. Gordon, *Ugaritic Textbook* (Rome: Pontifical Biblical Institute, 1965), 472ff.

7. See Ahiqar 71:5, 28 in A.E. Cowley *Aramaic Papyri of the 5th Century BC* (Oxford: The Clarendon Press, 1923), 178-80.

8. Ahiqar 126, 128, 167. In Cowley, 216, 218.

9. Whitley, 469, 475.

10. Olley, 15.

11. George A. Cooke, *A Text-Book of North-Semitic Inscriptions* (Oxford: The Clarendon Press, 1903), 86.

12. John Gray, "The Legacy of Canaan," Supp. to *VT* 5 (1957): 95.

13. M. Dunand, "Nouvelle Inscription Phoenicienne Archaique," *Revue Biblique*

39 (1930): 321-31.

14. Cooke, 18ff.

15. William Foxwell Albright, "The Phoenician Inscriptions of the Tenth Century BC from Byblos," *JAOS* 67 (1947): 156-57.

16. James Swetnam, "Some Observations on the Background of צַדִּיק in Jeremiah 23:5a," *Biblica* 46 (1965): 29-40, especially 34-35. See also "wbn ṣdq ytnmlk" ('and the legitimate heir, Ytnmlk'), and "wlṣmḥ ṣdq" ('and for the legitimate offspring'). As for 'righteousness' see "bṣdqy wbḥkmty" ('because of my righteousness and my wisdom') in R.S. Tomback, *A Comparative Semitic Lexicon of the Phoenician and Punic Languages* (Missoula: Scholars Press, 1978), 277. Cooke translates here 'righteousness' too. Cooke, 180-81.

17. Swetnam, 36 and note 2. In thirteen Nabatean tomb inscriptions from El Hejra there is a repeated phrase אצדק באצדק which Cooke translates: 'each legal kinsman' in the sense of legal right. The prefix 'ב' of באצדק is distributive as in שנה בשׁנה ('each year'—Deut. 15:20), so it would mean 'each heir in turn.' Swetnam sees a connection between this צדק of the first century and the post-exilic Hebrew צדק in the meaning of 'genuine,' 'legitimate.' For example, the phrase גֵּר צדק and its synonym גֵּר אמת ('genuine proselyte'), כֹּהֵן צדק ('legitimate priest') and משׁיח צדק ('legitimate High Priest').

18. Julian Oberman, *Ugaritic Mythology* (New Haven: Yale University Press, 1948), 29, note 30.

19. Other relevant passages are: Prov. 25:5, Ps. 89:15. How can Jehoiachin be the subject of this prophecy, while Jeremiah says והקמתי, that is, he refers to a future king, to an unknown offspring, at an unknown date? This is probably the same king about whom Isaiah prophesies in 9:6. The question of legitimacy is not raised, neither here nor in Isaiah. Jeremiah stresses the issue of justice and ethics three times in two verses (5-6) as against רע מעלליהם ('wicked acts')

of the present leaders (v. 2).

20. Mitchell Dahood, *Proverbs and Northwest Semitic Philology* (Roma: Pontificum Institutum Biblicum, 1963), 15.

21. A.R. Gordon, "Righteousness," *Encyclopedia of Religion and Ethics*, edited by James Hastings (New York: Charles Scribner's Sons, 1951), X: 780-84.

22. Roy A. Rosenberg, "The God Ṣedeq," *HUCA* 36 (1965), 162.

23. Snaith, 72.

CHAPTER 2

1. Snaith, 72. However, he deals with them separately in some cases and discerns quite a difference in meaning.

2. Snaith, 73.

3. Snaith, 72-76.

4. James E. Priest, *Government and Judicial Ethics in the Bible and Rabbinic Literature* (New York: Ktav Publishing, 1980), 104-49.

5. Herbert B. Huffmon, *Amorite Personal Names in the Mari Texts* (Baltimore: Johns Hopkins Press, 1965), 256.

6. Eliezer Berkovits, "The Biblical Meaning of Justice," *Judaism* 18 (Spring 1969): 188-209.

7. Gordon, 780, 782.

8. Sawyer, *Semantics*, 50, 59.

9. John H. Bollier, "The Righteousness of God," *Interpretation* 8 (1954): 404.

10. Elizabeth Rice Achtemeier, "Righteousness in the O.T.," *IDB* 4 (1962): 80-81.

11. Heinz H. Schrey, et al., *The Biblical Doctrine of Justice and Law* (London: SCM Press, 1955), 66-79.

12. Edmond Jacob, *Theology of the O.T.*, trans. A.W. Heathcote and P. J. Allcock (New York: Harper Press, 1958), 94ff.

13. Johannes Pedersen, *Israel, Its Life and Culture* (London: Oxford University Press, [1926] 1954), 338ff.

14. Whitley, 475.

15. *BDB* (Oxford: The Clarendon Press, 1955), 841-42.

16. Yaacov Shalom Licht, "צדקה", *Encyclopedia Mikrait* (1971), VI: 678-81.

17. Snaith, 70-71. See also Ezek. 18: 19,21, Ps. 33:5.

18. Albert Léopold Vincent, *La Religion des Judéo-Araméens d'Élephantine* (Paris: P. Geuthner, 1937), 174, footnote 7.

19. Franz Rosenthal, "Sedaka, Charity," *HUCA* 23, Part I (1950-51): 419-30.

20. 1 Sam. 12:7, Micah 6:5, Ps. 103:6. See also chapter 9.

21. Snaith, 70-71.

22. Shalom Spiegel, *Amos vs. Amaziah*, Essays in Judaism Series, No. 3 (New York: Herbert H. Lehman Institute of Ethics, 1957), 33.

CHAPTER 3

1. Gordon, 78.

2. The preceding two chapters emphasize the abominations (תועבה) done by other nations. These abominations defile the land, the people and the *name* of God (18:21). Consequently, they were destroyed. The third collection of laws emphasizes the holiness of God and His people. Any diversion from the law defiles the divine holiness (19:8).

3. After Ibn Ezra, מקראות גדלות, נב.

4. If one regards these texts as pre-exilic.

5. Rashi noticed that. רש"י, מקראות גדלות, נד (ב). Martin Noth suggested that this statement "might well be a secondary addition." *Leviticus*, 2nd edition, translated by J.E. Anderson (Philadelphia: Westminster Press, 1977), 144.

6. Driver reads: 'and judge righteously (or righteousness).' Samuel Rolles Driver, *Deuteronomy*, 3rd edition, ICC (Edinburgh: T. & T. Clark, [1895] 1901), 286. The question I raise is: how can one judge righteousness? The 'righteousness' is not the object of the judging. The Hebrew phrase בין...ובין can be seen as a distributive expression, emphasizing that each person is equal in the eyes of the law.

7. Ezek. 18:8, Zech. 7:9.

8. Driver, too, reads צדק as adjective and translates: 'a whole and just stone.' driver, 286. So is Spiegel, 33.

9. The words שלמה and שלם in the meaning of 'perfect,' 'whole,' 'the way it should be,' are Deuteronomistic (1 Kgs. 6:7, 8:61, 15:14, 27:6). They are associated with אמת (2 Kgs. 20:3) as צדק is (Ps. 45:5, 85:15).

10. This repetitive style for emphasis is found also in 2:27: בְּדֶרֶךְ בְּדֶרֶךְ אֵלֵךְ—'only

on the road I will walk.' Here are additional functions of this style:

1. 'Very,' as in Qoh. 7:25: וְעָמֹק עָמֹק—'very deep'; Prov. 20:14: רַע רַע

—'very bad'; Isa. 50:4: בַּבֹּקֶר בַּבֹּקֶר—'in the very early morning.'

2. 'Every,' as in Isa. 58:2: יוֹם יוֹם—'every day'; Lev. 22:18, Ezek. 14:4: אִישׁ

אִישׁ—'every man'; Ezek. 21:14,33: חֶרֶב חֶרֶב—'every sword.'

3. Close to this meaning is 'time after time,' 'all your life,' as in צֶדֶק צֶדֶק

תִּרְדֹּף—'You shall pursue justice all your life,' according to Ibn Ezra, דברים

מִקְרָאֹת גְּדֹלוֹת (תש"א-1951): גמ (ב). This style conveys a sense of continuity.

4. To hurry up, to hasten the listeners for action, to stir emotions, as in Isa.

51:9,17: עוּרִי עוּרִי—'wake up! Wake up!' Also 52:11, 57:14, 62:10.

5. To emphasize the pronounced word, to leave a great impression on the

gravity and significance of the word, as in Isa. 57:19: שָׁלוֹם שָׁלוֹם—'Peace!

Peace!' Also, Lev. 13:45, Jer. 6:14, 8:11, Ezek. 16:23, 21:32.

11. See Jer. 22:29.

12. The repetition of the phrase אֲנִי ה' (e.g. 18:21, 19:3,12,14,16,36) underlines

the pure essence of God that stands in contradiction to any wrong doing.

Deviating from His laws defiles the people. The right to the land of Israel

comes from their being holy and separate from other nations (20:24,26).

CHAPTER 4

1. This poem is repeated in Ps. 18 which is probably a later version. There, צדק comes instead of צדקה. Perhaps that redactor thought that צדק was more appropriate, or that for him there was no difference between the two.

2. As a variant of אמונה, אמת parallels or functions as a synonym of צדקה often. צדק parallels אמונה (אמן) much more frequently. For example, Isa. 1:26, 59:4, Hos. 2:21-22, Prov. 12:17.

3. In 1 Sam. 24:17 and Ps. 142:8 the verb גמל in pa'al is associated with the word צדיק. In Gen. 50:15 and Joel 4:4 both verbs שוב and גמל appear together. The connection between being תמים ('perfect,' 'innocent'), the one who follows God's laws, and reward of longevity also appears in Ps. 119:1,17.

4. Judg. 6:7, 1 Sam. 7:8,9, 8:18.

5. רד"ק, שמואל, מקראות גדולות (ניו יורק: הוצאת חברת תנ"ך, 1959): קסח.

6. משה צבי סגל, ספרי שמואל (ירושלים: קרית ספר, 1968): שנג.

7. יהודה קיל, ספר שמואל (ב) (ירושלים: מוסד הרב קוק, תשמ"א-1981): תפו.

8. Henry Preserved Smith, *The Book of Samuel*, ICC (New York: Charles Scribner's Sons, [1899] 1901), 365.

9. משפט is the legality of an action or simply *the law*, as in Jer. 22:13.

10. On the meaning of משפט see Zeev W. Falk, "Two Symbols of Justice," *VT* 10 (1960): 72-74.

11. Micah (3:1) makes it very clear when he claims that the leaders of Israel know the law and its aspects, but nevertheless they distort its precepts (vv. 2-3,9-11).

12. The noun אמונה stems from the verb אמן, the masculine word for אמת—'truth.' Truth is what is correct, steadfast and factual.

13. רש"י, רמב"ן, בראשית, מקראות גדולות: לד (א-ב)

14. Ephraim Avigdor Speiser, *Genesis*, The Anchor Bible (Garden city: Doubleday, 1964), 110, 112.

15. Driver, *The Book of Genesis*, 2nd edition (London: Methuen & Co., 1904), 176.

16. John Skinner, *Genesis*, ICC (New York: C. Scribner's Sons, 1925), 280.

17. Driver, *Genesis*, 195.

18. Speiser, 132.

19. Skinner, 278.

20. Driver, *Genesis*, 392.

21. Speiser, 234.

22. See "קרא גמל המצות צדקה" :(ב) ב :מקראות גדולות, דברים, רמב"ן. According to Ramban צדקה is the outcome, the recompense a person gains by doing good deeds. It is the psychological good feeling and self-satisfaction one achieves from doing something good to someone else, especially if he is not required to do so. Ramban compares this reward to a master, having bought a slave to serve him, he rewards him for his work by paying him, although he is not obligated to do so.

23. Gerhard von Rad, *Deuteronomy, A Commentary*, The O.T. Library (London: SCM Press, 1966), trans. Dorothea Barton, 65.

24. Daniel (9:18) uses the same concept but a different style: כִּי לֹא עַל-צִדְקֹתֵינוּ כִּי עַל...אֲנַחְנוּ. In Deut. 9:5 the structure is: כִּי ב-...בְּצִדְקָתְךָ לֹא כִּי). The English translation remains the same. The literary style sounds like that of a confession of the accused before the judge. And this is how Daniel feels (v. 20).

25. The only time these three traits are mentioned together is in Deut. 32:4. There, God is צדיק וישר...[אמת= אמונה] אֵל אֱמוּנָה—'a truthful God...just and upright.' אמונה and צדקה are mentioned together in 1 Sam 26:23, 2 Sam. 22:21,25.

26. Reward usually pertains to prolonged life and salvation from enemies.

27. אבן עזרא, חזקוני, מקראות גדולות: פט (ב)

28. Lorin W. Batten, *The Books of Ezra and Nehemiah*, ICC (New York: C. Scribner's Sons, 1913), 204.

CHAPTER 5

1. It occurs in couplets: צדק ושלום (85:11), צדק ומשפט (89:15, 97:2), משפט וצדק (119:121), צדק חסד (7:9); in parallel with תמים (15:2), אמת (45:5), אמונה (96:13), רשע (45:8), שקר (52:5), מישרים (58:2), הקיץ (17:15), משפט (37:6), תהלה (35:28) and כבד (97:6). It also appears in phrases, such as: משפט צדק (five times in chapter 119), אמרת צדק (119:123), חפץ צדק (55:27), פועל צדק (15:2) and many more.

2. Charles Augustus Briggs, *The book of Psalms*, ICC (New York: C. Scribner's Sons, 1906-7)), 127.

3. אבן-עזרא, אונקלוס, תהלים, מקראות גדולות: ט

4. Dahood reads preposition 'ב' of בצדק as a "causal force." On the basis of Karatepe בצדק ובחכמתי ('because of my justice and my wisdom'), Panamuwa בצדק הושבני ('because of my justice [or legitimacy] he enthroned me') and Agbar בצדקתי קדמה ('because of my justice before him') he concludes that here, too, בצדק should be translated: 'I, because of (my) justice, shall behold your face.' Mitchell Dahood, "Qoheleth and Northwest Semitic Philology," *Biblica* 43 (1962): 359. Using צדק at the opening of the psalm may have been deliberately done in order to create an inclusio.

5. The idea itself is not clear. Ibn Ezra suggests that צדק is the philosophical ability to comprehend and enjoy God's creation. אבן-עזרא, תהלים, מקראות גדולות: ט (ב).

6. Dahood translates צדק 'pronounce just verdicts.' This I found after coming to the same conclusion on my own as shown above. Dahood does not explain how he came to this translation. Mitchell Dahood, *Psalms*, II, The Anchor Bible

(Garden city: Doubleday, 1968), 56, 57.

7. See also Isa. 45:23 and the discussion on page 126.

8. שׁד ושׁבר (Isa. 69:7), דת ודין (Esther 1:13) and more.

9. A slightly different interpretation will be offered later on page 45.

10. See also v. 18.

11. Mitchell Dahood, *Psalms*, I, The Anchor Bible (Garden City: Doubleday, 1966), 269, 272.

12. The same idea is found in Jer. 33:17-18.

13. 2 Chron. 6:41-42 is almost a duplicate of Ps. 132:8-10. The idea in Ps 132:12 is repeated in 2 Chron. 6:16. See also Isa. 61:10b. The conclusion is that Ps. 132 may be a post-exilic poem.

14. Either God or the righteous person is "clothed" with other positive attributes such as glory (Job 40:10), צדק—'justice' (Job 29:14), צדקה and vengeance (Isa. 59:17) and strength (Isa. 51:9, 52:1, Ps. 93:1). However, Hebrew uses this expression to express also negative characteristics, such as curses to come upon a person and curses to be despised, as in Ps. 109:18-19, shame and infamy (35:26, 109:29, 132:18, Job 8:22) and fear (Ezek. 26:16). It seems that the expression to wear a blessing or a curse comes from the post-exilic period.

15. Here a verb is missing like נֶהֱגִים ('are uttered') as in v. 7. The basic meaning of 'straight' for צדק is very clear. It contrasts that which is crooked and perverse. The idea is repeated also in v. 9b in the word יְשָׁרִים.

16. Rosenberg, 161-77.

17. Harold Henry Rowley, "Zadok and Nehushtan," *JBL* 58 (1939): 130-32.

18. Christian Ewing Hauer, "Who was Zadok?" *JBL* 82 (1963): 90.

19. Rosenberg, 163-64.

20. In Rosenberg's words: "Just as in Babylonia subordinate deities on occasion came to be regarded as parts of the body of the great God." Page 170.

21. Here יְמִינְךָ is the subject not צֶדֶק: 'Your right hand is filled with justice.'

22. The idea of Ṣedeq as deity is not original to Rosenberg. He quotes Mowinck-el's definition of "The Ṣedeq of Adonai" as this: "...a divine entity, partly a manifestation of a superior divinity. It represents the personification of a quality or an activity or a component part of the superior deity."

The Messopotamian and Canaanite gods were independent entities. When required they had to explain their actions to their superior gods, but never were they part of their superiors' body.

23. Also Ps. 97:2. If צדק is a god, so then is משפט, which is utterly false.

24. Rosenberg ignores the 'god' חסד. He probably could not find a Canaanite god by this name.

25. Rosenberg ignores the fact that עיר הצדק appear with a definite article and not as עיר צדק or קרית צדק. This עיר הצדק refer to בה ילין צדק משפט מלאתי (v. 21) that deals very clearly with justice and the law of the people. There is no need to read what is absent. Also, מַלְכִּי צדק and אֲדֹנִי צדק may have originally referred to a god צדק, but Isaiah refers to civil justice.

26. To follow his theory the phrase קריה נאמנה (the verb אמן being the masculine form of נאמן) refers to "the city of (the god) Amin."

27. He also mentions that in 50:7 Adonai is called מזה צדק. Rosenberg, 173-74. Did Jeremiah believe that Adonai's body was the habitation of Ṣedeq? It is preposterous and very unlikely.

28. In an intricate and interesting article Julian Morgenstern asserts that the original name of the Eastern Gate (The Golden Gate) was שַׁעֲרי צדק. The tradition concerning this gate was, already in Biblical times, that only the righteous will enter the Temple through them (Ps. 118:20). Furthermore, that the King of Glory enters through them (24:7-10). This is 'כבוד ה whom Ezekiel envisions leaving and returning to the Temple through שער הקדים, the Eastern Gate (11:1,23, 43:1-2,4).

On the two equinoctial days of the year, which fall in autumn and spring, the rays of the rising sun hit the gates. On these two days only these gates would open to celebrants. The eastern Gate was then already built as two gates, as Jeremiah (7:2b) and Psalms (24:7-10) prove. The belief was that these gates were indestructible, עולם פתחי ('eternal gates'), and that is why Jeremiah found it significant to prophecy the destruction of the Temple while standing at the gate.

There was a time when the people worshipped the sun, facing the gate, with their back to the Temple (Ezek. 8:16). This gate was also called שער החרסית ('the Pottery Gate'—19:2). Julian Morgenstern, "The Gates of "Righteousness," *HUCA* 6 (1929): 1-37.

29. Whitley, 469-75.

30. See also קטב ('scourge'—Ps. 91:6), עברה ('wrath'), זעם ('indignation'), צרה ('trouble'), מות ('death') and דבר ('pestilence') in Ps. 78:49-50.

31. Ytb krt l'dh ytb lks' mlk – 'Krt sits upon his seat, he sits upon his royal throne.' Also Ps. 89:30,39, 93:5, 60:11, 110:1. See Dahood, *Psalms*, II, 81.

32. Moses Buttenwieser, *The Psalms* (New York: Ktav Publishing House, 1969), 401, 403:405.

33. Dahood, *Psalms*, II, 2, 10. Mitchell Dahood, *Psalms*, I, The Anchor Bible (Garden City: Doubleday, 1966), 25.

34. Roger T. O'Callaghan, "Echoes of Canaanite Literature in the Psalms," *VT* 4 (1954): 170.

35. אבן-עזרא, תהלים, מקראות גדלות: ג.

36. Snaith, 73.

37. See Isa. 31:4, 43:7.

38. Gen. 22:2, 1 Kgs. 14:23, Jer. 2:20.

39. Rad, 203.

40. This is the transliteration of the Hebrew מַלְכִּי-צֶדֶק. However, whenever I quote a commentator, his variant will be used.

41. Mitchell Dahood, *Psalms*, III, The Anchor Bible (Garden City: Doubleday, 1970), 112, 117-81.

42. There are commentators who read צדק-מלכי as other than a proper name. For example, R. H. Smith in his article "Abram and Melchizedek (Gen. 14:18-20)," *ZAW* 77 (1965): 146 and Amos Hakham in his commentary on Psalms ספר תהלים עג-קנ (ירושלים: מוסד הרב קוק, 1981):‏ שם. Hakham suggests that מלכי-צדק could be a title for a righteous king.

43. Buttenwieser, 794-96.

44. A. Joseph Fitzmyer, "Further light on Melkizedek from Qumran Cave 11," *JBL* 86 (1967): 25-41.

45. Cf. 1 Sam. 2:7-8 where the suffix yohd does not appear.

46. As in Deut. 22:24, 23:5, 2 Sam. 13:22.

47. אבן-עזרא, תהלים, מקראות גדלות: עא (ב).

48. They suggest that most likely Zadoq represented the Aaronid cultic center in Hebron (see Josh. 21:11, 1 Chron. 6:40, Num. 26:58a where Hebron is mentioned as a home for early priestly families). Frank Moore Cross, *Canaanite Myth and Hebrew Epic* (Cambridge, Mass. and London, 1973), 206-15. Menahem Haran, "Studies in the Account of the Levitical Cities, II," *JBL* 80 (1961): 156-65, especially 160-61.

49. Saul Olyan, "Zadok's Origins and the Tribal Politics of David," *JBL* 101 (1981): 177-93.

50. John G. Gammie, "Loci of the Melchizedek Tradition of Gen. 14:18-20," *JBL* 90 (1971): 395-406, note 54. He bases his theory on other scholars who located Melchizedek's tradition in various centers like Shechem, Tabor and Shiloh.

51. Dahood wrongly translates 'gates of victory.' The emphasis put on the gates is that of righteousness not of wars. He separates שערי צדק (the town gates through which the army passes) from זה השער in v. 20 (the gate of the

Temple). *Psalms*, III, 159.

52. Buttenwieser, 662.

53. Also Isa. 26:7 where מעגל צדיק parallel ארח מישרים. In 59:8 the sinners have no משפט in their path. They twist their ways. In Prov. 2:9 מעגל טוב is a summation of צדק משפט ומישרים וכל מעגל טוב ('rightness and justice and equity —every good course'). In 2:18-20 רפאים מעגלותיה ('her course leads to the shades') are the opposite of ארחות חיים ('the paths of life'), דרך טובים ('the path of the good') and ארחות צדיקים ('the paths of the righteous').

54. Spiegel translates: 'He leads me in a straight path.' Page 33.

55. Robert B.Y. Scott, *Proverbs*, The Anchor Bible (Garden City: Doubleday, 1965), 104.

56. As suggested by William McKane in *Proverbs* (Philadelphia: Westminster Press, 1970), 493. See a similar structure in v. 17: מסלת ישרים...שמר נפשו... ('the highway of the upright...he who preserves his life...).

57. A similar idea appears in Zophar's speech, in Job 11:14: 'If there be iniquity in your hand, get it away from you, let no wickedness dwell in your tent. Then you will be able to lift your face free from blemish. You will be firmly set with nothing to fear.' This firmness will constitute a shield against misery, hopelessness and the wicked (vv. 16-20).

58. In Proverbs it seems that מישרים has nothing to do with the law. It is another term for ישר מעגלי or ישר ארחות. מסלת ישרים—straight or honest ways—are the opposite of ארחות עקשים—'the paths of the crooked' (2:15). There are those who emend מישרים to read תָּאֵשַׁר, יָאַשֵׁר or יְאַשֵׁר. There is no need for this, since it is repeated in 1:2. Also, מישרים appears three more times, twice referring to the drunkard who 'talk מישרים' (23:31).

59. In old Wisdom the emphasis was on the discipline of piety rather than on the educational discipline.

60. McKane, 283.

61. McKane, 222.

62. Scott, 67

63. Crawford H. Toy, *Proverbs*, ICC (New York: C. Scribner's Sons, 1899), 166.

64. Toy, 539.

65. McKane, 260.

66. Scott, 183.

67. The words עול, עולה appear in Proverbs as opposites to צדק (29:27) and to טוב (22:23).

68. The feminine form of מח, as in Ps. 68:13 and Zeph. 2:6.

69. The notion that a place obtains its name from the people who use it is expressed also in the epithets שערי צדק and עיר הצדק.

70. So does George A. Barton in *The Book of Ecclesiastes*, ICC (New York: C. Scribner's Sons, 1909), 125.

71. Robert B.Y. Scott, *Ecclesiastes*, The Anchor Bible (Garden City: Doubleday, 1965), 222.

72. A. Lukyn Williams, *Ecclesiastes*, The Cambridge Bible (Cambridge: University Press, 1922), 42, 43. I find this to be a very good definition where righteousness is connected with the forensic aspect of justice. Nonetheless, in 5:7 he translates צדק—'justice.'

73. I quote Meir Zlotowitz in *Ecclesiastes* (New York: ArtScroll Studios, Ltd., 1976), 91. However, I was unable to find anything in Sforno resembling this.

74. רש"י, קהלת, מקראות גדולות: צד (ב)

75. Deuteronomy associates the adherence to the law with longevity (11:8-9, 30:20, 32:46-47). This is a further confirmation for the influence of Wisdom on the Deuteronomistic literature as promoted by Moshe Weinfeld.

76. In Job 'straight' (ישר) parallels צדק indirectly through the root תם/תמם (1:1, 22:3, 9:20, 27:5-6). However, these idea and connection appear also in Psalms (25:21, 37:37) and in Proverbs (11:3, where חמת ישרים interchange with צדקה

יְשָׁרִים in v. 6). In any case, Job prefers the word תֻּמָּה as a synonym for צֶדֶק (2:3,9, 27:5, 31:6) to יָשָׁר or יָשָׁר. He uses the word תָּם to denote 'a straight person,' the equivalent of the word צַדִּיק the prophets use (1:1,8, 2:3, 8:20-22) and תֹּם in the same sense of 'a straight way' (4:6, 21:23). Proverbs does the same with the words תֹּם and תֻּמָּה (2:7, 10:9, 11:3, 13:6, 19:1, 20:7, 28:6).

CHAPTER 6

1. As Thomas K. Cheyne suggests in *The Book of Psalms* (London: Kegan Paul, Trench & Co., 1884), 216.

2. See *Biblica Hebraica*, ed. Rudolf Kittel, 7th edition, 1951, 979.

3. Franciscus Zorell, *Zorell Lexicon Hebraicum* (Roma: Pontificum Institutum Biblicum, 1965), 684a.

4. Dahood, *Psalms*, I, 28, 33-34, 146, 150-51.

5. According to Dahood מישׂר and אֶרֶץ in 67:5 are separated by תנחם as a double-duty verb, thus reading: 'You will lead nations into the plain (במישׂר), and peoples into the land (בארץ),' namely, Paradise.

   This interpretation is incorrect for (ב)מישׂר is connected with עמים תשׁפט. The word בארץ goes back to v. 3 where דרכך refers to ישׁעתך. God will lead the nations in His path on earth so that all will enjoy His salvation. Why will they be happy and saved? Because they will realize that God judges all nations equally with the right, straight laws (במישׁר). The outcome of this acknowledgement is being blessed (vv. 2,8) and the earth will be blessed for man's sake (v. 7). The word מישׂר in 67:5 has nothing to do with Paradise but with justice. The blessing will not occur in heaven but here on earth.

6. השׁיעני בחסדך (Ps. 31:17), בצדקתך פלטני (v. 2), באמונתך ענני בצדקתך (143:1).

7. The psalmist of 142 hopes that when saved he will be put in the land of life—אֶרֶץ החיים (vv. 6-7).

8. עמים חכם, ספר תהלים א-עב (ירושלים: מוסד הרב קוק, 1979), ת

9. See Ps. 143:11b-12a.

10. McKane, 223, 350. See also 245, 556.

11. Scott translates צדקה דֶּרֶך—'life of virtue.' *Proverbs*, 106.

12. On Maat see Henry Frankfort's *Ancient Egyptian Religion* (New York: Harper and Row, [1948] 1961), especially 43-77.

13. The description of דֹּרֶך צדקה (21:21) or מַעְגְּלֵי צדקה is found in Ps. 112.

14. Dahood moves from 'fidelity' to 'faithful deeds' and 'faithful acts.' *Psalms*, II, 170-71.

15. Dahood translates again 'generosity.' *Psalms*, I, 217.

16. As Dahood translates. He sees no parallelism here and translates צדקה as 'generosity' in the meaning of blessings and good deeds. *Psalms*, II, 309.

17. The idea of peace and goodness being declared from the mountains is found in Isa. 52:7. See also Nahum 2:1.

18. Dahood, *Psalms*, II, 180, 125.

19. A similar idea is found in Qoh. 11:1: שלח לחמך על-פני המים כי-ברב הימים תמצאנו—'Send your bread forth upon the waters; for after many days you will find it.'

20. Read חָסֶר ('disgrace' or 'impoverishment') for חֹסֶר after LXX. If חסר is correct then a negative word like בְלֹא is missing (13:23, 16:8, 19:2, Qoh. 7:17, Ps. 17:1, 44:13). Another instance, where a negative word dropped, is found in v. 33: תִּוָּדַע (לא).

21. As translated by Robert Gordis in *Poets, Prophets and Sages* (Bloomington: Indiana University Press, 1971), 410. Translations by Buttenwieser, Driver-Gray and Hakham read רֹב צדקה as a continuation of the description of God's qualities, who abounds in righteousness, who does not pervert justice or subvert a man in his cause.

    יְעַנֶּה may mean either 'afflict' or 'answer' man's questions (if it is unvocalized). Samuel Rolles Driver, George B. Gray, *The Book of Job*, ICC (Edinburgh: T. & T. Clark, 1921), 324. Buttenwieser translates: 'He that abboundeth in righteousness gives no accounting.' Moses Buttenwieser, *The*

Book of Job (New York: The MacMillan Co., 1922), 144, 283. He reads יַעֲנֶה, as substantiated by the Greek translation, which parallels it to מְצָאֻנוּ. It was deliberately changed to avoid Job's declaration that God does not answer. Hakham understands יַעֲנֶה as Gordis but ascribes רֹב צדקה to God, who does not enjoy tormenting people. עמום חכם, ספר איוב (ירושלים: מוסד הרב קוק, 1970), רפז.

22. 34:10b-12,17-29.

23. Driver-Gray, 304.

24. The verb חרף appears only here in Job. The noun חרפה appears twice, in 16:10 and in 19:5. In 16:10 Job's enemies smote his cheeks in *an act of hatred*: בחרפה הכו לחיי. In 19:4-5 Job brings up the possibility that he may have erred He addresses his friends and challenges them to prove his *mistakes*: ותוכיחו עלי חרפתי. The first meaning suits better our passage than the second: Job swears that his heart did not harbor any hatred. בצדקתי stands as the opposite of יחרף לבבי, meaning: 'to my clean, righteous behavior I have held fast.'

25. Gordis, 364, 379.

CHAPTER 7

1. Snaith, 69-70, 76.

2. Snaith, 59.

3. Olley, 16.

4. Olley, 112.

5. Whitley, 469-75.

6. Ed Nielsen, "The Righteous and the Wicked in Habaqquq," *Studia Theologica* 6 (1953): 54-73.

7. Swetnam, 38.

8. A.R. Gordon, 780-84.

9. Rosenberg, 161-77, especially 171.

10. Spiegel, 52-56.

11. This assertion is incorrect. רשעה/רשע are opposites of צדקה/צדק. He quotes Amos as evidence for his theory that פשע is connected to the covenant. However, all those פשעים ('crimes') mentioned in 1:3-2:4 concern ethical sins of other nations who have no covenant with God. These are universal ethical laws of behavior. In other quotations פשע is not mentioned at all. Bollier, 404-409.

12. Achtemeier, 83-85.

13. Schrey et al, 51-53.

14. Schrey et al, 58ff.

15. Isa. 32:1, 11:5, 26:9, Ps. 72:2.

16. Cf. 4:3, 9:5, 19:18, 48:1,5, Zech. 8:3.

17. Olley, following his theory, says that when a king wears צדק and אמונה he faithfully fulfills the covenant, thus bringing harmony, balance and peace to his society as well as to nature. Olley, 95.

18. תרגום, רש"י, קמחי, ישעיהו, מקראות גדולות: כב (א-ב)

19. So is Edward J. Kissane in *The Book of Isaiah* (Dublin: Brown & Nolan Ltd., The Richview Press, 1960), 179, 185: 'excels in righteousness'; Luzzatto explains מהר צדק: בקי ומרגל לעשות צדק ('competent and in the habit of doing what is just'). שמואל דוד לוצטו, ספר ישעיהו (פדובה: 1855), 204. See the phrase ספר מהיר in Ps. 45:2, Ezek. 7:6, and איש מהיר in Prov. 22:29.

20. So is Skinner who translates: 'swift to do righteousness.' He also suggests 'expert in justice.' John Skinner, *Isaiah 1-39*, The Cambridge Bible (Cambridge: University Press, [1896] 1930), 138; G.W. Wade suggests similarly in *The Book of the Prophet Isaiah* (London: Methuen and Co. 1929), 112; Herbert translates: 'swift to do right.' Arthur Sumner Herbert, *Isaiah 1-39* (Cambridge: University Press, 1973), 109; Cheyne translates: 'prompt in righteousness.' Thomas K. Cheyne, *The Prophecies of Isaiah*, 3rd edition (New York: Thomas Whittaker, 1884), 101; Kimhi explains: זריז ומהיר —'swift and prompt.' דוד קמחי, ישעיהו, מקראות גדולות: כח.

21. Translation of the Hebrew Scriptures by the Jewish Publication Society of America (JPS).

22. Gen. 18:7, 41:32, Judg. 9:48, Esther 5:5, Mal. 3:5. Also note Targum's ויעבד.

23. Luzzatto, 204.

24. Haplography of בַּל because of תֵּבֵל.

25. George B. Gray, *The Book of Isaiah 1-39*, ICC (New York: C. Scribner's Sons, 1912), 441-43.

26. רד"ק, ישעיהו, מקראות גדולות: לט (ב)

27. That may be only one literary style found also in other passages, e.g.

26:14,18, 33:23. However, triplets are also used, e.g. in 33:20, 44:9, or quadruplets, as in our passage (if we accept the accidental omission) in 44:8-9. Sometimes it parallels another negative word like לא as in 20:21 and Prov. 12:3.

28. Ps. 118:22.

29. E.g. Gen. 2:7, 12:1, 23:17-18.

30. See Dahood, *Psalms*, III, xxix, xxvii; E.g. Ps. 31:3 להושעי.

31. O. Procksch, *Hosea*, Biblica Hebraica, ed. Rudolf Kittel, 7th edition, 1951.

32. As described in Deut. 11:13-15.

33. Francis I. Andersen and David N. Freedman, *Hosea*, The Anchor Bible (Garden City: Doubleday, 1980), 417, 425, 560. Also Gordis translates similarly. Gordis, 28. However, in p. 310 he suggests the second interpretation where יורה צדק mean 'teach you righteousness.'

34. According to James Luther Mays. *Hosea*, The O.T. Library (Philadelphia: Westminster Press, 1969), 147.

35. So does Cheyne: 'till he come and rain righteousness.' צדק is God's gift of salvation, being the divine principle of righteousness in action. Thomas K. Cheyne, *Hosea* (Cambridge: The University Press [1899] 1913), 106; See also William R. Harper, *Amos & Hosea*, ICC (New York:C. Scribner's Sons, 1905), 356 and 38 (תש"ט), חש"ט דביר: הוצאת דביר (תל-אביב: מזבה, עמס, הושע, יוסף הרדי; George A. Knight, *Hosea, God's Love* (London: SCM Press, 1967), 106.

36. Translated by Dahood, *Psalms*, I, 281. See *ANET*, 136ff.

37. T. Worden, "The Literary Influence of the Ugaritic Fertility Myth on the O.T.," *VT* 3 (1953): 273-97.

38. Martin J. Buss, *The Prophetic Word of Hosea* (Berlin: Verlag Alfred Topelmann, 1969), 106-07.

39. Hans Walter Wolff, *Hosea*, trans. Gary Stansel (Philadelphia: Fortress Press, 1974), 180.

40. Harper, 356, 357.

41. עמיאל הלפרן, <u>הושע, נסיון של באור חדש</u> (ירושלים: החברה לחקר המקרא בישראל),
214.

42. James M. Ward, *Hosea, A Theological Commentary* (New York: Harper and Row, 1966), 176.

43. רש"י, <u>הושע</u>, מקראות גדולות: צו (ב).

44. The closest to this interpretation is McKeating who translates: 'just measure of rain.' Henry McKeating, *The Books of Amos, Hosea and Micah* (Cambridge: University Press, 1971), 134.

45. See also פנ, (1973 ,קק הרב מסד הוצאת :ירושלים) <u>הושע ספר</u> ,קיל יהודה

46. They also appear as parallels in Isaiah, Jeremiah and Proverbs.

47. Harper argues that בצדק ובמשפט are a gloss. Harper, 242. Mays and Wolff translate צדק as 'saving help of God' or 'salvation,' although no threat from within or without is alluded to. Mays, 51, Wolff, 46. The word במשפט and the context of divine attributes exclude any such connotation.

48. John M.P. Smith, William H. Ward, Julius A. Bewer, *Micah, Zephaniah, Nahum, Habakkuk, Obadiah and Joel*, ICC (Edinburgh: T. & T. Clark, 1912), 214-51.

49. John Bright, *Jeremiah*, The Anchor Bible (Garden City: Doubleday, 1965), 84.

50. Samuel Rolles Driver, *The Book of the Prophet Jeremiah* (New York: C. Scribner's Sons, [1892] 1906), 70. So is Elliott L. Binns, *The Book of the Prophet Jeremiah* (London: Methuen & Co. Ltd., 1919), 108.

51. Sheldon Blank, *Jeremiah Man and Prophet* (Cincinnati: Hebrew Union College Press, 1961), 108, 113, 119.

52. Elmer A. Leslie, *Jeremiah* (Nashville: Abigdon Press, 1954), 326.

53. Ernst W. Nicholson, *The Book of the Prophet Jeremiah 26-52* (Cambridge: University Press, 1975), 67. He also suggests to translate: 'O home of righteousness.'

54. רד"ק, יִרְמְיָהוּ, מִקְרָאוֹת גְּדוֹלוֹת: קמ.

55. In Ezra 10:2 and 1 Chron. 29:15 מִקְוֶה means simply 'hope,' with no reference to God. Jeremiah twice uses the word תִּקְוָה as 'hope.'

56. The English language is unable to convey this double message.

57. On this issue see, יחזקן אהרוני, "הַוֵּי בָּנֶה בֵּיתוֹ בְלֹא־צֶדֶק," עיונים בַּסֵּפֶר יִרְמְיָהוּ חֵלֶק ב' (1971), 56-75 (יְרוּשָׁלַיִם: דְּבָרֵי חוּג הָעִיּוּן בְּתַנַ"ךְ בְּבֵית נְשִׂיא הַמְּדִינָה).

58. Bright, 137.

59. The Syriac, Targum, Vulgate and the Aquila translations read יִקָּרֵאהוּ ('he will be called'). The Syriac and Vulgate read similarly in 33:16. Targum reads שְׁמָהּ ('her name'). In some Hebrew manuscripts the word is יִקְרְאוּ ('they will call') and יִקְרָאֻהָ ('they will call her') referring to Jerusalem. Targum explains ה' צִדְקֵנוּ (33:16): 'rights will be rendered to us before God inside her,' that is, inside the city of Jerusalem. In 23:6 Targum refers the name to the king (בְּיוֹמוֹהִי—'in his days'). Kimhi follows this translation in both texts: the people of Jerusalem will say: "Adonai is our justice." The Messiah's name will reflect reality: as long as he lives, justice will rule and God will constitute the people's provision.

60. Bright, 144.

61. See J. Gerald Janzen, *Studies in the Text of Jeremiah* (Cambridge, Mass.: Harvard University Press, 1973), 31-32.

62. 3:19: אָבִי.

63. Deut. 28:10, 1 Kgs. 8:43, Jer. 7:10,11,14,30, 14:9, 15:16, 25:29, Dan. 9:19, Isa. 61:3, 62:2-4,12, 63:19. The idea that in the days to come there will be changes in names is evident in Hosea and Isaiah as well.

64. Jeremiah confers another name for Jerusalem: כִּסֵּא ה' (3:17).

65. Another synonym for the verbs רדף and בקש is דרש (Zeph. 1:6, Judg. 6:29, Isa. 55:6).

66. Christopher R. North, *The Second Isaiah* (Oxford: Clarendon Press, 1964),

208, 210.

67. Olley, 98-102.

68. See 56:1, 57:5-7 (idol worship), 58:6-7,9b-10a,13 (keeping the Sabbath), 59:3-8,13-15 (crimes and injustice). Actually, keeping the legal laws of the teaching is being ethical.

69. Perhaps the letter 'נ' of נשׁפט was copied twice because of the 'נ' of אָז.

70. Ps. 37 is dependent heavily on Wisdom literature and Deutero-Isaiah. See, for example, v. 2 (Isa. 40:7-8), vv. 22a,26b,29a (Isa. 60:21a, 61:9b), v. 28a (Isa. 61:8a).

71. An extension of this idea is found in 60:1-3.

72. E.g., Leslie, 233.

73. Solomon Freehof, *The Book of Isaiah* (New York: Union of American Hebrew Congregations, 1972), 318.

74. James D. Smart, *History and Theology in Second Isaiah* (Philadelphia: Westminster Press, 1965), 272.

75. See also Josh. 6:9, 2 Sam. 10:9.

76. Whitley, 472-73. Similarly, Morgenstern translates בצדק: 'with sure purpose.' Julian Morgenstern, *The Message of Deutero-Isaiah in its Sequential Unfolding* (Cincinnati: Hebrew Union College Press, 1961), 149, 150, 152.

77. Smart, 66-69.

78. The sun-god was the god of justice.

79. The verb עוד also means 'to overcome' as in 64:6, Job 17:8.

80. Ps. 18:39, 110:1, 1 Kgs. 5:17, or 'control' as in Isa. 66:1.

81. Luzzatto, 456-57.

82. Smart, 93.

83. Edward J. Young, *The Book of Isaiah*, III (Grand Rapids: Eerdmans, 1972), 134.

84. Ps. 52:5, 12:17.

85. In the same meaning as Ps. 40:10.

86. דבר נבלה ('he who speaks impiety'—Isa. 9:16), דבר מישרים ('he who speaks uprightly'—33:15), דברי כזב ('they who speak lies'—Ps. 5:7, 58:4), דבר אמת ('he who speaks the truth'—15:2), דברי שלום ('they who speak peace'—28:3), דבר ישרים ('he who speaks honestly'—Prov. 16:13).

87. Smart, 126.

88. John Skinner, *Isaiah 40-66*, The Cambridge Bible (Cambridge: University Press [1896] 1930), 72.

89. Wade, 297.

90. This he bases on passages like Judg. 3:10, 4:4, 2 Kgs. 15:5, Isa. 40:23, Ps. 2:10 and Job 36:27ff. H.L. Ginsberg, "A Strand in the Cord of Hebraic Hymnody," *Eretz Israel* 9 (1968): 46-47.

91. Knight, 136.

92. Reuben Levy, *Deutero-Isaiah* (London: Oxford University Press, 1925), 187.

93. Whitley, 472.

94. John L. McKenzie, *Second Isaiah*, The Anchor Bible (Garden City: Double-day, 1968), 118. So does Leslie although he translates צדק as 'deliverance.' Leslie, 187.

95. Ginsberg, 47.

96. Isa. 61:8, Jer. 32:40, Ezek. 16:60, 37:26.

97. David Syme Russell, *Daniel* (Edinburgh: The Saint Andrew Press and Philadelphia: Westminster Press, 1981), 184-85.

98. E.W. Heaton, *The Book of Daniel* (London: SCM Press, 1956), 212.

99. Samuel Rolles Driver, *The Book of Daniel* (Cambridge: University Press, 1901), 136.

CHAPTER 8

1. *Isaiah* (Philadelphia: The Jewish Publication Society, 1973), 394.

2. משה גרשן-גוטשטיין, <u>ספר ישעיה</u> (ירושלים: האוניברסיטה העברית, תשל"ה), מב

3. Bollier, 406.

4. רש"י, <u>ישעיה</u>, מקראות גדולות: כא

5. 28:2,17b, 30:25,28,30, 23:11a, 8:7-8. The imagery of flowing, or rapid and imminent disaster is also used figuratively of a whip (28:15,18), shelter (28:17) and of a spirit (30:28).

6. 'To walk in righteousness' conveys the meaning of 'to do righteous acts.'

7. Luzzatto, 381.

8. Herbert, 188.

9. As summarized in 33:15: הלך צדקות ודבר מישרים ('He who performs righteous deeds and speaks the truth').

10. Or, as seen above, v. 28 contrasts only צדקה.

11. תרגום, רד"ק, <u>ישעיה</u>, מקראות גדולות: ד

12. C. von Orelli, *The Prophecies of Isaiah* (Edinburgh: T. & T. Clark, 1889), 20.

13. Exod. 3:9, Ps. 9:13, Isa. 19:20, Job 34:28 and many more.

14. If we accept that the Priestly source is a later literature.

15. Snaith, 51ff.

16. 33:5.

17. Also 2:11,17, 33:5.

18. Leslie, 33-34.

19. Luzzatto, 76.

20. Kimhi sees the sanctification among the evil who, having been punished, would

acknowledge His holiness and supremacy as the Superior Judge.

21. McKeating, 42.

22. Compare 'my fruit' (of Wisdom) where צדקה is one of its components (Prov. 8:18-19).

23. James Luther Mays, *Amos*, The O.T. Library (Philadelphia: Westminster Press, 1969), 92-93.

24. Hans Walter Wolff, *Joel and Amos* (Philadelphia: Fortress Press, 1977), 245-46.

25. This reading is strengthened by verses like Ps. 7:9, 37:9, 18:21,25, Jer. 51:10, 1 Sam. 26:23, 2 Sam. 22:21,25, 1 Kgs. 8:32.

26. Bollier, 406.

27. This is how JPS translates חסד, 783.

28. Mays, *Hosea*, 146.

29. McKeating, 134.

30. Buss, 21, 106, 107.

31. As Targum, Symmachus and Vulgate translate. So does Rashi explain.

32. Wolff, *Joel*, 55.

33. Julius A. Bewer, *Joel*, ICC (Edinburgh: T. & T. Clark, 1912), 115-16.

34. Solomon Freehof, *Book of Jeremiah* (New York: Union of American Hebrew congregations, 1977), 74-75.

35. Moses Buttenwieser, *The Prophets of Israel* (New York: MacMillan Co., 1914), 145, note 2.

36. Nicholson, 86.

37. Ginsberg, 48.

38. Rudolf Kittel, *Biblia Hebraica*, 7th edition, 1951.

39. Dahood, *Psalms*, II, 5 (note on 51:9).

40. Dahood, *Psalms*, II, 1.

41. Knight finds that צדק relates to divine acts and צדקה—to human, although its

source is divine too. This righteousness, he says, is the human exhibit of compassionate love. George A. Knight, *Deutero-Isaiah: a Theological Commentary on Isaiah 40-55* (New York: Abingdon Press, 1965), 136.

42. McKenzie, 78; Cheyne, *Isaiah*, 294.

43. North, 152.

44. Luzzatto, 507.

45. Similar is 59:20.

46. The word ישועה is a feminine form but the letter 'י' (like ישע) makes it appear and sound masculine. The letter 'ת' is a feminine prefix although not in the case of ישע, since there is no תֵּשַׁע. See 59:16 where צדקה and ישועה appear alongside נכם (masculine) and קנאה (feminine).

47. See דֹחת עולמם in v. 9, 57:16, 34:10.

48. Rosenberg, 172.

49. Olley, 84.

50. The words שם, תהלה and תפארת appear together in Jer. 13:11, 33:9, Deut. 22:19. שם and תהלה appear together in Zeph. 3:19,20, Isa. 48:9 (כבד is added in v. 11), Ps. 48:11, while כבד and תהלה appear together in Isa. 42:8, Ps. 66:2.

51. Cheyne, *Isaiah*, II, 102. So is Skinner, *Isaiah*, II, 195.

52. W. Emery Barnes, *Haggai, Zechariah and Malachi*, The Cambridge Bible (Cambridge: University Press, 1934), 65.

53. Mitchell, G. Hinckley et al, *Haggai, Zechariah, Malachi and Jonah*, ICC (Edinburgh: T. & T. Clark, 1912), 208.

54. מרדכי זר-כבוד, זכריה, תרי עשר כרך ב' (ירושלים: מוסד הרב קוק, 1976), ל.

55. John P.M. Smith, *The Book of Malachi*, ICC (Edinburgh: T. & T. Clark, 1912), 64-65.

56. Rex Mason, *Haggai, Zechariah and Malachi* (Cambridge, N.Y.: Cambridge University Press, 1977), 151.

57. זר-בבד, יג

58. רד"ק מלאכי, מקראות גדלות: קסו (ב)

59. J.M.P. Smith, 80.

60. זר-בבד, יר

61. A.R. Gordon, 782.

62. Mason, 158.

63. Raymond Hammer, *The Book of Daniel* (Cambridge, N.Y.: Cambridge University Press, 1976), 97.

64. Heaton, 207.

65. Russell, 176-77.

66. André Lacocque, *The Book of Daniel*, trans. David Pellauer (Atlanta: John Knox Press, 1979), 185.

67. M. Delcor, *Le Livre de Daniel* (Paris: J. Gabalda, 1971), 198.

68. Louis F. Hartman, *The Book of Daniel*, The Anchor Bible (Garden City: Doubleday, 1978), 239, 243.

CHAPTER 9

1. Norman K. Gottwald, *The Tribes of Yahweh* (New York: Orbis Books, 1979), especially 117-119; *The Hebrew Bible, A Socio-Literary Introduction* (Philadelphia: Fortress Press, 1985), especially 271.

2. Leonard L. Thompson, "The Jordan Crossing: Ṣidqot Yahweh and World Building," *JBL* 100 (September 1981), 352-358.

CHAPTER 10

1. As Snaith concluded regarding the word צֶדֶק. However, as found here, this definition applies only to צְדָקָה.

2. Ezekiel has no specific term for the divine justice. For him 'רוּחַ ה ('the spirit of Adonai') is the force which will descend from God to fill up man's heart, so that man will be motivated to do justice (11:19-20, 18:31, 36:26-27). He probably replaces Jeremiah's idea of implanting the spirit of God into the corrupt practiced law. This is the force that causes the historical saving acts of God. Micah, Deutero-Isaiah and Daniel call this force צְדָקָה while Deutero-Isaiah uses צֶדֶק as that divine attribute of justice. For Isaiah that spirit is also the force that causes man to do justice (11:5). Deutero-Isaiah and Micah link it also to the knowledge of justice (Isa. 40:13-14, Micah 3:8). Moreover, Micah connects it with the retribution measures taken by God (2:7).

3. On the influence of Wisdom on the prophets see, for instance, Hans Walter Wolff's *Amos the Prophet*, trans. Foster R. McCurley (Philadelphia: Fortress Press, 1973). Read especially the editor's introduction by John Reumann.

4. There are only three possible cases: in Isa. 5:23 it seems that it should have been צֶדֶק צַדִּיקִם instead of צִדְקַת צַדִּיקִם which sounds better. צֶדֶק, in its juristic meaning, is more appropriate. The choice of צְדָקָה over צֶדֶק is done for stylistic purposes only. In Jer. 51:10 צִדְקֹתֵינוּ may have originally been צִדְקָתֵינוּ. Only in Micah צְדָקָה means 'innocence' which can very well be a poetic preference. צֶדֶק clearly means 'vindication' or 'innocence' in Psalms and Deutero-Isaiah.

5. E.g. Deut. 11:14-15,21,23-25, 28:1-13.

6. Hos. 10:12, Ps. 72:1-2, 98:2,9, 119:142, Jer. 22:13,15, 23:5-6, 33:15-16, Isa. 45:8,19,23, 51:5-6,7-8, 58:2,8 and perhaps Dan. 9:7,24.

BIBLIOGRAPHY

I list here the books, articles and entries that have been of use in the making of this book. However, some of the writings I have consulted are listed here although they are not quoted in this study.

Achtemeier, Elizabeth Rice. "Righteousness in the O.T." *IDB*, 1962, IV, 80-85.

Albright, William Foxwell. "The Phoenician Inscriptions of the Tenth Century B.C. from Byblos." *JAOS* 67 (1947): 153-60.

Anderson, Francis I. and Freedman David N. *Hosea*. The Anchor Bible. Garden City, N.Y.: Doubleday, 1980.

Ball, Charles J. *The Prophecies of Jeremiah*. New York: A.C. Armstrong and Son, 1890.

Barnes, Emery W. *Haggai, Zechariah and Malachi*. The Cambridge Bible. Cambridge: The University Press, 1934.

Barr, James. *Comparative Philology and the Text of the Old Testament*. Oxford: Clarendon Press, 1968.

Barton, George A. *The Book of Ecclesiastes*. ICC. New York: C. Scribner's Sons, 1909.

Batten, Loring W. *The Books of Ezra and Nehemiah*. ICC. New York: C. Scribner's Sons, 1913.

Bennett, William H. *The Book of Jeremiah*. New York: A.C. Armstrong and Son, 1895.

Berkovits, Eliezer. "The Biblical Meaning of Justice." *Judaism* 18 (Spring 1960):

188-209.

Bewer, Julius A. *Joel*. ICC. Edinburgh: T. & T. Clark, 1912.

Binns, Elliott L. *The Book of the Prophet Jeremiah*. London: Methuen & Co. Ltd.,
1919.

Blank, Sheldon H. *Jeremiah Man and Prophet*. Cincinnati: Hebrew Union College
Press, 1961.

Bloomfield, Leonard. *Language*. New York: H. Holt & Co., 1961.

Bollier, John H. "The Righteousness of God." *Interpretation* 8 (1954): 404-13.

Briggs, Charles Augustus. *The Book of Psalms*. ICC. New York: C. Scribner's
Sons, 1906-1907.

Bright, John. *Jeremiah*. The Anchor Bible. Garden City, N.Y.: Doubleday, 1965.

Buss Martin J. *The Prophetic Word of Hosea*. Berlin: Verlag Alfred Topelmann,
1969.

Buttenwieser, Moses. *The Book of Job*. New York: The MacMillan Co., 1922.

——— . *The Prophets of Israel*. New York: MacMillan Co., 1914.

——— . *The Psalms*. New York: Ktav Publishing House, 1969.

Campbell, Edward F. "The Amarna Letters and the Amarna Period." *BA* 23
(February 1960): 2-22.

Cheyne, Thomas K. *Hosea*. Cambridge: The University Press, (1899) 1913.

——— . *The Book of Psalms*. London: Kegan Paul, Trench & Co., 1884.

——— . *The Prophecies of Isaiah*. 3rd edition. New York: Thomas Whittaker, 1884.

Collinson, W.E. *Comparative Synonyms: Some Principles and Illustrations*.
Transactions of the Philological Society, 1939.

Cook, Stanley A. *The Truth of the Bible*. London, 1938.

Cooke, George A. *A Text-Book of North-Semitic Inscriptions*. Oxford: The
Clarendon Press, 1903.

——— . *The Book of Ezekiel*. ICC. Edinburgh: T. & T. Clark, 1951.

Cowley, Arthur E. *Aramaic Papyri of the 5th Century B.C.* Oxford: The Clarendon Press, 1923.

Crenshaw, James L. "Popular questioning of the Justice of God in Ancient Israel." *ZAW* 82 (1970): 380-95.

Cross, Frank Moore. *Canaanite Myth and Hebrew Epic.* Cambridge, Mass. & London, 1973.

Cunliff-Jones, Herbert. *The Book of Jeremiah.* New York: MacMillan, 1960.

Dahood, Mitchell. *Proverbs and Northwest Semitic Philology.* Roma: Pontificum Institutum Biblicum, 1963.

——. *Psalms.* I. The Anchor Bible. Garden City, N.Y.: Doubleday, 1966.

——. *Psalms.* II. The Anchor Bible. Garden City, N.Y.: Doubleday, 1968.

——. *Psalms.* III. The Anchor bible. Garden City, N.Y.: Doubleday, 1970.

——. "Qoheleth and Northwest Semitic Philology." *Biblica* 43 (1962): 349-65.

Davidson, Andrew Bruce. *Ezekiel.* Cambridge: The University Press, 1916.

Delcor, M. *Le Livre de Daniel.* Paris: J. Gaalda, 1971.

Driver, Samuel Rolles. *Deuteronomy.* ICC. Edinburgh: T. & T. Clark, (1895) 1901.

——. *The Book of Daniel.* Cambridge: The University Press, 1901.

——. *The Book of Genesis.* Westminster Commentaries. 2nd edition. London: Methuen & Co., 1904.

——. *The Book of the Prophet Jeremiah.* New York: C. Scribner's Sons, 1892) 1906.

Driver, Samuel Rolles, Gray, George Buchanan. *The Book of Job.* ICC. Edinburgh:: T. & T. Clark, 1921.

Falk, Zeev W. "Two Symbols of Justice." *VT* 10 (1960): 72-74.

Fitzmyer, Joseph A. "Further Light on Melkizedek from Qumran Cave 11." *JBL* 86 (1967): 25-41.

Fohrer, Georg. "The Righteous Man in Job 31." *Essays in O.T. Ethics*. Edited by
    James L. Crenshaw and John T. Willis. New york: Ktav Publishing House,
    1974: 1-21.

Frankfort, Henry. *Ancient Egyptian Religion*. New York: Harper and Row, (1948)
    1961.

Freedman, Harry. *Jeremiah*. London: The Soncino Press, 1949.

Freehof, Solomon. *The Book of Ezekiel*. New York: Union of American Hebrew
    Congregations, 1978.

——. *The Book of Isaiah*. New York: Union of American Hebrew Congregations,
    1972.

——. *Book of Jeremiah*. New York: Union of American Hebrew Congregations,
    1977.

Gammie, John G. "Loci of the Melchizedek Tradition of Gen. 14:18-20." *JBL* 90
    (1971): 385-96.

Ginsberg, H.L. "A Strand in the Cord of Hebraic Hymnody." *Eretz Israel* 9
    (1969): 45-50.

Gordis, Robert. *Poets, Prophets and Sages*. Bloomington: Indiana University
    Press, 1971.

——. *The Book of Job*. New York: Jewish Theological Seminary of America,
    1978.

Gordon, A.R. "Righteousness (in the O.T.)." *Encyclopedia of Religion and Ethics*.
    Edited by J. Hastings. X, 780a-84a. New York: C. Scribner's Sons, 1951.

Gordon, Cyrus H. *Ugaritic Textbook*. Roma: Pontifical Biblical Institute, 1965.

Gottwald, Norman K. *The Hebrew Bible, A Socio-Literary Introduction*. Phila-
    delphia: Fortress Press, 1985.

——. *The Tribe of Yahweh*. New York: Orbis Books, 1979.

Gray, George B. *The Book of Isaiah 1-39*. ICC. New York: C. Scribner's Sons,
    1912.

Gray, John. "The Legacy of Canaan." Supp. *VT* 5 (1957).

Hammer, Raymond. *The Book of Daniel*. Cambridge, N.Y.: Cambridge University Press, 1976.

Haran, Menachem. "Studies in the Account of the Levitical Cities, II." *JBL* 80 (1961): 156-65.

Harper, William R. *Amos and Hosea*. ICC. New York: C. Scribner's Sons, 1905.

Hartman, Louis F. *The Book of Daniel*. The Anchor Bible. Garden City, N.Y.: Doubleday, 1978.

Hauer, Christian Ewing. "Who was Zadok?" *JBL* 82 (1963): 89-94.

Heaton, E.W. *The Book of Daniel*. London: SCM Press, 1956.

Herbert, Arthur Sumner. *Isaiah 1-39*. Cambridge: The University Press, 1973.

Huffmon, Herbert B. *Amorite Personal Names in the Mari Texts*. Baltimore: John Hopkins Press, 1965.

Irwin, William A. "Job's Redeemer." *JBL* 81 1962): 217-29.

Jacob, Edmond. *Theology of the O.T.* Translated by A.W. Heathcote and P.J. Allcock. New York: Harper Press, 1958.

Janzen, Gerald J. *Studies in the Text of Jeremiah*. Cambridge, Mass.: Harvard University Press, 1973.

Kaiser, Otto. *Isaiah 13-39*. The O.T. Library. Philadelphia: Westminster Press, 1974.

Kissane, Edward J. *The Book of Isaiah*. Dublin: Brown & Nolan Ltd. The Richview Press, 1960.

Knight, George A.F. *Deutero-Isaiah: A Theological Commentary on Isaiah 40-55*. New York: Abingdon Press, 1965.

——— . *Hosea; God's Love*. London: SCM Press, 1966.

Kraeling, Emil G. *Commentary on the Prophets*. Camden: T. Nelson, 1966.

Lacocque, André. *The Book of Daniel*. Translated by David Pellauer. Atlanta: John

Knox Press, 1979.

Lambert, W.G. *Babylonian Wisdom Literature*. Oxford: Clarendon Press, 1960.

Leslie, Elmer A. *Jeremiah*. Nashville: Abingdon Press, 1954.

Levy, Reuben. *Deutero-Isaiah*. London: Oxford University Press, 1925.

Mason, Rex. *Haggai, Zechariah and Malachi*. Cambridge, N.Y.: Cambridge University Press, 1977.

Mauchline, John. *Isaiah 1-39*. London: SCM Press, 1962.

Mays, James L. *Amos*. The O.T. Library. Philadelphia: Westminster Press, 1969.

——. *Hosea*. The O.T. Library. Philadelphia: Westminster Press, 1969.

McKane, William. *Proverbs*. The O.T. Library. Philadelphia: Westminster Press, 1970.

McKeating, Henry. *The Books of amos, Hosea and Micah*. Cambridge: The University Press, 1971.

McKenzie, John L. *Second Isaiah*. The Anchor Bible. Garden City, N.Y.: Doubleday, 1968.

Mitchell G. Hinckley et al. *Haggai, Zechariah, Malachi and Jonah*. ICC. Edinburgh: T. & T. Clark, 1912.

Montgomery, James A. *The Book of Daniel*. ICC. New York: C. Scribner's Sons, 1927.

Morgenstern, Julian. "The Gates of Righteousness." *HUCA* 6 (1929): 1-37.

——. *The Message of Deutero-Isaiah in its Sequential Unfolding*. Cincinnati: Hebrew Union College Press, 1964.

Nicholson, Ernst W. *The Book of the Prophet Jeremiah 26-52*. Cambridge: The University Press, 1975.

Nielsen, Ed. "The Righteous and the Wicked in Habaqquq." *Studia Theologica* 6 (1953): 54-78.

North, Christopher R. *The Second Isaiah*. Oxford: Clarendon Press, 1964.

Noth, Martin. *Leviticus*. 2nd edition. Translated by J.E. Anderson. Philadelphia: Westminster Press, 1965.

Oberman, Julian. *Ugaritic Mythology*. New Haven: Yale University Press, 1948.

O'Callaghan, Roger T. "Echoes of Canaanite Literature in the Psalms." *VT* 4 (1954): 164-76.

Olley, John W. *"Righteousness" in the Septuagint of Isaiah: A Contextual Study*. Missoula: Scholars Press, 1979.

Olyan, Saul. "Zadok's Origins and the Tribal Politics of David." *JBL* 101 (June 1982): 177-93.

Orelli, C. von. *The Prophecies of Isaiah*. Translated by J.S. Banks. Edinburgh: T. & T. Clark, 1889.

Pedersen, Johannes J. *Israel, Its Life and Culture*. London: Oxford University Press, (1926) 1954.

Porteus, Norman W. *Daniel*. The O.T. Library. Philadelphia: Westminster Press, 1965.

Priest, James E. *Government and Judicial Ethics in the Bible and Rabbinic Literature*. New York: Ktav Publishing House, 1980.

Rad, Gerhard von. *Deuteronomy: A Commentary*. Translated by Dorothea Barton. The O.T. Library. London: SCM Press, 1966.

Redpath, Henry A. *The Book of the Prophet Ezekiel*. New York: Edwin S. Gorham, 1907.

Rosenberg, Roy A. "The God Ṣedeq." *HUCA* 36 (1965): 161-77.

Rosenthal, Franz. "Ṣedaka, Charity." *HUCA* 23, Part I (1950-51): 411-30.

Rowley, Harold Henry. "Zadok and Nehushtan." *JBL* 58 (1939): 113-41.

Russell, David Syme. *Daniel*. Edinburgh: The Saint Andrew Press and Philadelphia: Westminster Press, 1981.

Ryle, Herbert E. *The Books of Ezra and Nehemiah*. Cambridge: Cambridge

University Press, (1897) 1923.

Sawyer, John F. *A Modern Introduction to Biblical Hebrew*. Boston: Oriel Press, 1976.

———. *Semantics in Biblical Research*. SBT 2/24, 1972.

Scholnick, Sylvia Huberman. "The Meaning of Mišpat in the Book of Job." *JBL* 101 (4), (1982): 521-29.

Schrey, Heinz H., Walz, H.H., Whitehouse, W.A. *The Biblical Doctrine of Justice and Law*. London: SCM Press, 1955.

Scott, Robert B.Y. *Proverbs, Ecclesiastes*. The Anchor Bible. Garden City, N.Y.: Doubleday, 1965.

Skinner, John. *Genesis*. ICC. New York: C. Scribner's Sons, 1925.

———. *Isaiah 1-39; 40-66*. The Cambridge Bible. Cambridge: The University Press, (1896) 1930.

Smart, james D. *History and Theology in Second Isaiah*. Philadelphia: The Westminster Press, 1965.

Smith, George A. *The Book of Isaiah*. London: Hodder and Stoughton, (1892) 1900.

Smith, Henry Preserved. *The Book of Samuel*. ICC. New York: C. Scribner's sons, (1899) 1909.

Smith, John M.P. *The Book of Malachi*. ICC. Edinburgh: T. & T. Clark, 1912.

Smith, John M.P., Ward, William H., Bewer, Julius A. *Micah, Zephaniah, Nahum, Habakkuk, Obadiah and Joel*. ICC. Edinburgh: T. & T. Clark, 1912.

Smith, R.H. "Abram and Melchizedek (Gen. 14:18-20)." *ZAW* 77 (1965): 129-52.

Snaith, Norman H. *The Distinctive Ideas of the Old Testament*. London: The Epworth Press, 1944.

Speiser, Ephraim Avigdor. *Genesis*. The Anchor Bible. Garden city, N.Y.: Doubleday, 1964.

Spiegel, Shalom. *Amos Vs. Amaziah*. New York: Herbert H. Hehman Institute of
Ethics, 1957.

Streane, Annsley William. *Jeremiah*. Cambridge: Cambridge University Press,
(1913) 1926.

Streane, Annsley William, Davidson, Andrew Bruce. *Ezekiel*. Cambridge:
Cambridge University Press, 1924.

Swetnam, James. "Some Observations on the Background of צַדִּיק in Jeremias
23:5a." *Biblica* 46 (1965): 29-40.

Thompson, Leonard L. "The Jordan Crossing: Ṣidqot Yahweh and World
Building." *JBL* 100 (September 1981): 343-58.

Tomback, R.S. *A Comparative Semitic Lexicon of the Phoenician and Punic
Languages*. Missoula: Scholars Press, 1978.

Toy, Crawford H. *Proverbs*. ICC. New York: C. Scribner's Sons, 1899.

Ullmann, Stephen. *Semantics*. New York: Barnes and Noble, 1962.

Unger, Merrill F. *Zechariah*. Grand Rapids: Zondervan Publishing House, 1970.

Wade, G.W. *The Book of the Prophet Isaiah*. London: Methuen and Co., 1929.

Ward, James M. *Hosea*. New York: Harper and Row, 1966.

Waterman, Leroy. "Note on Job 19:23-27: Job's Triumph of Faith." *JBL* 69
(1950): 379-80.

Weiser, Artur. *The Psalms*. Philadelphia: Westminster Press, 1962.

Whitley, C.F. "Deutero-Isaiah's Interpretation of Ṣedeq." *VT* 22 (October 1972):
469-75.

Williams, Lukyn A. *Ecclesiastes*. The Cambridge Bible. Cambridge: The
University Press, 1922.

Wolff, Hans Walter. *Amos the Prophet*. Translated by Foster R. McCurley.
Philadelphia: Fortress Press, 1973.

——— . *Hosea*. Translated by Gary Stansel. Philadelphia: Fortress Press, 1974.

——— . *Joel and Amos*. Philadelphia: Fortress Press, 1977.

Worden, T. "The Literary Influence of the Ugaritic Fertility Myth on the O.T." *VT* 3 (1953): 273-97.

Young, Edward J. *The Book of Isaiah*. III. Grand Rapids: Eerdmans, 1972.

"צֶדֶק, צְדָקָה." *Zorell Lexicon Hebraicum et Aramaicum*. Roma: Pontificum Institutum Biblicum, 1965: 682b-84b.

Zimmerli, Walther. *Ezekiel 1-24*. Translated by Ronald E. Clements. Philadelphia: Fortress Press, 1979.

Zink, James K. "Impatient Job." *JBL* 84 (1965): 147-52.

Zlotowitz, Meir. *Ecclesiastes*. New York: ArtScroll Studios, Ltd., 1976.

HEBREW
BIBLIOGRAPHY

אבישור. יצחק. "וכליותי אשתונן (תה׳ עג.כא). למשמעות הפועל שנ"ן בעברית ובאוגרית." <u>לשוננו</u> 44/4 (תמוז תש"מ): 263-267.

אהרוני. יוחנן. "הוי בנה ביתו בלא-צדק." <u>עיונים בספר ירמיהו.</u> חלק ב׳. ירושלים: דברי חוג העיון בתנ"ך בבית נשיא המדינה (1971): 53-67.

בן-חיים. זאב. "השורש ערב. הכלול בו והנלוה עמו." <u>לשוננו</u> 44 (טבת תש"מ): 85-99.

ברוזניק. נחום. "הסמנטיקה של השורש חלש להסתעפויותיו." <u>לשוננו</u> 41 (ניסן תשל"ז): 163-175.

ברנר. עתליה. "על מטה ושבט וסיווגן הסמנטי." <u>לשוננו</u> 44/2 (טבת תש"מ): 100-108.

גושן-גוטשטיין. משה. <u>ספר ישעיהו.</u> ירושלים: הוצאת האוניברסיטה העברית. תשל"ה.

הלפרן. עמנואל. <u>הושע. נסיון של ביאור חדש.</u> ירושלים: החברה לחקר המקרא בישראל. 1976.

הררי. יוסף. <u>עמוס. הושע. מיכה.</u> תל-אביב: הוצאת דביר. תשי"ט.

זר-כבור. מרדכי. <u>זכריה.</u> תרי-עשר כרך ב׳. ירושלים: מוסד הרב קוק. 1976.

חכם. עמוס. <u>ספר איוב.</u> ירושלים: מוסד הרב קוק. 1970.

---. ‫ספר תהלים. א-עב‬. ירושלים: מוסד הרב קוק. 1979.

---. ‫ספר תהלים.עג-קנ‬. ירושלים: מוסד הרב קוק. 1981.

לוצטו. שמואל דוד. ‫ספר ישעיהו‬. פדובה. 1855.

ליכט. יעקב שלום. "צדק. צדקה." ‫אנציקלופדיה מקראית‬. VI (1971):
      678-685.

מורג. שלמה. "שדי תרומת" (שמ"ב 1:21) - ביטוי מוזר." ‫לשוננו‬ 45
      (ניסן-תמוז תשמ"א): 317-318.

‫מקראות גדולות‬. ניו-יורק: הוצאת פרדס. תשי"א (1951).

קיל. יהודה. ‫ספר הושע‬. תרי-עשר כרך א׳. ירושלים: מוסד הרב קוק.
      1973.

רובינשטיין. אליעזר. "שלח-שילח. עיון תחבירי וסמנטי בלשון המקרא."
      ‫לשוננו‬ 38 (תשל"ד): 11-32.

ABBREVIATIONS

ANET - *Ancient Near Eastern Texts Relating to the O.T.* 2nd edition. Princeton: Princeton University Press, 1955.

BA - *The Biblical Archaeologist.* New Haven: The American Schools of Oriental Research.

BDB - Brown, F., Driver, S.R., Briggs, C.A. *Hebrew and English Lexicon of the Old Testament.* Oxford: The Clarendon Press, 1955.

cf. - Compare.

ff. - Following page(s), verse(s), etc.

HUCA - *Hebrew Union College Annual.* Philadelphia: The Jewish Publication Society.

ICC - *The International Critical Commentary.* New York: C. Scribner's Sons; Edinburgh: T. & T. Clark.

IDB - *The Interpreter's Dictionary of the Bible.* In four volumes. New York: Abingdon Press, 1962.

JAOS - *Journal of the American Oriental Society.* New Haven: The American Oriental Society.

JBL - *Journal of Biblical Literature.* Philadelphia: The Society of Biblical Literature and Exegesis.

JPS - Jewish Publication Society. The New Translation of the Hebrew Scriptures in three volumes: Torah (1962), Nevi'im (1978), Kethubim (1982). Philadelphia: The Jewish Publication Society of America.

LXX - The Septuagint Greek Version of the OT.

SBL - Society of Biblical Literature. A publication society. Montana: Scholars

Press.

SBT - *Studies in Biblical Theology*. London: SCM Press.

UAHC - Union of American Hebrew Congregations. A publication society.

VT - *Vetus Testamentum*. Leiden: E.J. Brill.

VT Supp. - *Vetus Testamentum Supplements*.

ZAW - *Zeitschrift fur die Alttestamentliche Wissenschaft*. Berlin: Walter de Gruyter
& Co.